Mumpreneurs
How to Juggle the Struggle

Labosshy Mayooran

Disdaimer

This book is designed to provide information and motivation to our readers. It is sold with the understanding that the author and publisher are not engaged to render any type of psychological, legal, or any other kind of professional advice. The content is the sole expression and opinion of its author. Neither the publisher nor the individual author(s) shall be liable for any physical, psychological, emotional, financial, or commercial damages, including, but not limited to, special, incidental, consequential or other damages. Our views and rights are the same: You are responsible for your own choices, actions and results.

All images in the book have been obtained from Pixabay free images gallery.

PUBLISHED BY DVG STAR PUBLISHING

NO PART OF THIS WORK MAY BE REPRODUCED OR STORED IN AN INFORMATIONAL RETRIEVAL SYSTEM, WITHOUT THE EXPRESS PERMISSION OF THE PUBLISHER IN WRITING.

www.mumpreneursbook.com

www.universallearningacademy.com

DEDICATION

Dedicated to my loving boys, Jaison and Mylesh,
all the inspirational mumpreneurs,
as well as the stay-at-home and working mums.

YOU ALL ARE TRULY INSPIRATIONAL!

CONTENTS

FOREWORD

Being Selfless begins with motherhood, the sum of all love. When you become a mother, your child becomes your universe. I remember the day my first child arrived, and it was the happiest day of my life. With each child comes a blessing and my three children helped me understand what living in the present moment really means and discover Inner Peace. Children leave no room for yesterday or tomorrow, all is happening now. Where is this new reality leaving you, as an aspiring young woman once you become a mother? What is happening with your future?

Labosshy Mayooran's book "Mumpreneurs", holds the answer! I want to warn you, this is not just another book about motherhood, but an entire new concept, an extraordinary solution to brilliancy and motherhood to co-exist and thrive.

When I first met Labosshy, she was a young, vibrant entrepreneur, with big dreams, with limitless creativity and unconditional love for others. Now, Labosshy is the happy mother of two beautiful boys (Jaison and Mylesh) and a very successful entrepreneur. What it takes to thrive, to achieve professional success, while raising your children?

If you are a mother and have big dreams, if you feel overwhelmed with motherhood and professional commitments, this book provides a much-needed solution to all the challenges of modern motherhood. I wish this book was written three decades ago!

Labosshy takes you into the "juggle the struggle" adventure and while the content is filled with techniques and key strategies you could apply immediately in your day to day life, her book is a golden guide on how to overcome the challenges you face as a Mumpreneur.

My favorite part is the creative brainstorming tool S.C.A.M.P.E.R and how it had been modified to fit the needs of mumpreneurs. It's definitely a method that will be useful to many mums.

As a final benefit Labosshy has provided some useful organizers that can be freely printed by following the simple instructions in the book. The motivational quotes and the chapter on affirmations truly put into perspective the true meaning of gratitude. After all, a successful life is not about what you receive, or you don't receive in life, but what you do about what you receive or you don't receive in life.

Not only I enjoyed reading this book, but Labosshy inspired me to plan a series of success stories on Mumpreneurs in Sovereign, global magazine for Executives and Leading Entrepreneurs

Dr Marina Nani
Founder of Radio W.O.R.K.S. World
Chief Editor, The Quantum of Light and Sovereign
www.RadioWorks.World

FEEDBACK & TESTIMONIALS

"Mumpreneurs - How to Juggle the Struggle in my view is essential reading for all parents. Labosshy's book seeks to expands your awareness upon how you could overcome the challenges that you face as a mumpreneur by providing you with both thought provoking and practical solutions. After all SHIFT HAPPENS whether we are aware of it or not. The question is, now that you have been exposed to the powerful teachings within these pages what POSITIVE SHIFT WILL HAPPEN FOR YOU NOW?"

– Sabrina Ben-Salmi
(BSc, mother of Fantastic 5, author, business/personal development consultant)

"THIS IS A MUST READ FOR ALL BUSY MUMS! The Men can learn from this as well to please your darling wife/partner!"

- Philip Chan
(10 seconds math expert, international speaker, double amazon bestseller and award winning author)

"Labosshy Mayooran brings you a BOOK that could be exactly what you need to end the struggles controlling your entrepreneurial life when you become a mum."

- Philip Oladejo (Founder of REAL D.A.D)

"Being a mother myself, this book has really been useful with many great solutions that you can put to use in your daily routines. Highly recommend this book to all parents."

- Salma Afshar
(Mother of twin boys and a baby girl)

This book is a must read for all mumpreneurs, stay-at-home and working mums. As a mum-to-be this book has come in very useful with excellent strategies on how to juggle the struggle."

- Erin Anthonyrajah
(BSc Hons, MSc, DIC, PhD Biochemistry)

As Labosshy's mother I am extremely proud of how far she has come. This book truly puts into perspective the struggles that parents go through to raise their children trying to juggle both work and family life.

- Ranjinidevi Sriskandarajah
(Labosshy's mother)

The book was a great read. I was inspired by the S.C.A.M.P.E.R tool and was intrigued by how it was applied. Extrememly proud of Labosshy. Definitely an essential read!

- Malini Senthilmani
(Labosshy's mother-in-law)

ACKNOWLEDGMENTS

I would like to express my gratitude and appreciation to my husband Mayooran Senthilmani, who inspired and motivated me to write this book. I also can't forget my lovely boys, Jaison and Mylesh; without them I would not have been writing this book today.

My sincere thanks goes out to....

Dr Marina Nani (Founder of Radio W.O.R.K.S. World Chief Editor, The Quantum of Light and Sovereign) for her kind words and support.

Prasanthika Mihirani (Founder of Swiss Creations) for my creative book cover design.

My Editors for the editing of my book, Dayna and the other who wishes to remain anonymous.

DVG Star Publishing for the publication.

Philip Chan, Philip Oladejo, Sabrina Ben-Salmi, Salma Afshar, Erin Anthonyrajah, Ranjini Sriskandarajah and Malini Senthilmani for their lovely testimonials.

I am very grateful to all the lovely mums who took time out of their busy schedules to contribute their personal stories to the chapter "Inspirational Mumpreneurs – the inside story". The contributors are Sabrina Ben-Salmi, Arabi Karteepan, Rushani Mahendran, Prasanthika Mihirani, Afia Miah, Victoria Parker, Fiona Seigneur, Victoria Fellowes and Kenny Akindele-Akande.

My special thanks go out to my parents who have raised me to be the person I am today whilst working to build a better life for my brother and me.

I am truly grateful and privileged to have such wonderful family, friends and colleagues in my life who have been extremely supportive throughout the process of writing this book.

"YOU ONLY LIVE YOUR LIFE ONCE, SO MAKE IT A MEMORABLE AND WORTHWHILE EXPERIENCE."

~CHAPTER 1~

INSPIRATIONAL JOURNEY

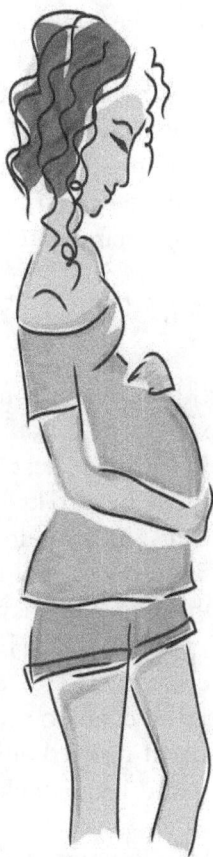

As a mother of two adorably handsome young boys, I know how it feels to have to struggle to just get through one day. There will be a thousand and one tasks that need to be done before the end of the day but there just isn't enough time. Everything just seems to be piling on top of one another, pile up on pile but never ending. Trust me ladies, I've been there, done that and I'm not denying it: it is and will be a struggle but please don't fret! There is a way you can get through the day without feeling so overworked and tired, but more energized and motivated. The solution is here!

This book will enable all mumpreneurs out there who either run their own business, go to work full-time or part-time, and even the stay-at-home mums (who are also valued for their unconditional hard work and sacrifice) to feel energized, organized and balanced in their day to day lifestyle.

MY STORY

In 2015 I had my first son, Jaison, and I was overwhelmed with joy and full of excitement to look after such a cute and adorable bundle of joy. I had the best 9 months of maternity leave where I tried my utter best to keep on top of things and purely focused on feeding and looking after my little one. As it grew closer to the time that I had to go back to work, it started to hit me: "Oh my gosh, I have to go back to work and leave my baby". I was so used to being around him 24/7 that it was just too emotional. However, I knew this day would come so I drafted an email to my manager, sending her the official day I'd be back. I sorted out childcare and was all organized and ready to start being back at work.

The day came and it was so emotional. I said bye bye to my little one as my husband dropped him off at nursery and I drove into work. To some extent I quite enjoyed going to work after so long, as it allowed me to have my own 'me time'. Being at work allowed me to unwind myself, have a different atmosphere, and I felt I was more connected with the outside world.

However, a month after I started work everything spiraled out of control. My son kept on getting ill and my husband and I found that we were taking time off work to stay at home and look after the little one. Week after week my son kept on getting some sort of cold and we'd get a phone call from the nursery to come and pick him up as he had a fever or loose stools. This continued for a couple of months. This situation was starting to put a strain on our family life as well as work. I had been promoted at work after my return from maternity leave so I really wanted to give it a shot and ensure that I didn't miss the opportunity to progress in my career. So I accepted and hoped that everything would work out in the long run.

Quite the contrary, there were nights after we had both gotten back from work when my son felt unwell with a high fever. We ended up having to call 111 and went to the out-of-hours urgent GP clinic. The whole night was spent with us having to see the doctor and getting my son assessed. By the time we got home it was time for us to be back at work. The number of countless times this happened led to sleep deprivation. We literally felt like zombies.

One day, on the way to work I had an accident with a lorry. Thankfully everyone was fine, however this was my breaking point. Both my husband and I thought enough is enough; this was a sign from GOD telling us to slow down. Together we made the decision that I would be a stay-at-home mum.

A couple of months along the line I started to think, what was I doing with my life? I spent most of my life in education, I had an MRes degree in Translational Medicine

3

from Imperial College London and a BSc (Hons) degree in Biomedical Sciences from Queen Mary University London, yet I wasn't using the things I had learnt to my full potential. I wanted my boys to look back and say proudly to others that their mother had achieved something. I wanted to inspire them to be the best they could be, but I had to show them how and be a role model. So my husband and I decided that we would set up our own business under the name 'Universal Learning Academy', which is an online learning platform, and that's how I became a mumpreneur.

Universal Learning Academy was formed in 2015 with the objective of creating a learning platform where everyone can learn anything. We started this pro-actively, thinking of creating something great during my time off from work to look after my kids. Currently we have 20,000 plus Facebook fans and it continues to grow every day. Our website has more than 100,000 visitors per month and is continuously growing. Our target is to create useful content to increase the number of visitors to our website and therefore the website's value will also increase. We managed to get two offers from companies in the USA to buy our website. We declined those offers because we are confident the value will rapidly increase by the end of 2018. We have published a number of books and online courses. We are also working with a number of like-minded people on joint venture projects to create digital products.

I am very excited about this new journey because it doesn't feel like I'm actually working. There's no need for me to wake up early to commute into work, and best of all, I get the opportunity to spend quality time with my kids.

Having gone through all three stages from being a working mum, stay-at-home mum to finally a mumpreneur, I can assure you that they all come with their own fair share of challenges.

Even though in this modern day maternity rights and flexible working opportunities make the workplace more accommodating, for us new mums it's still really difficult for us to achieve a satisfying work/life balance.

When I returned to work I constantly felt torn between not being there for my child and not feeling fully committed to my employer. Along with the high cost of childcare, it just didn't seem worthwhile. Staying at home can be more of an economical choice for some families rather than paying for childcare.

It was a tough decision to make when I finally decided to resign from my job and become a stay-at-home mum. Of course, we had to think things through financially, as the two-person income was cut down to one paycheck that our whole family had to live on. That's when I found sticking to a family budget was crucial. The economics of coupons, budgets and cutting corners were no longer optional. Having a husband who was encouraging and supportive of the idea made the transition so much easier. Most importantly, you can't put a price tag on physically being present for your children whilst watching them achieve their first milestones such as first steps, first words and so on.

When I became a stay-at-home mum, most people in our community thought that I was living a life of luxury with no job, no boss and no workplace stress. However it was quite the contrary. Yes, you're always available for your children, but always being there can sometimes feel as if you're trapped. I loved being a stay-at-home mum but there were times when I wished I could steal some time for myself. I eliminated the feeling of isolation by taking my sons to play groups where we got to interact with other mums as well as attending baby massage and yoga classes. On the weekends we went out as a family, taking our sons to swimming classes which allowed us to spend quality time as a family.

Even though my husband is the world's best teammate, I sometimes tend to feel that I need to do all the household chores (seeing as I'm home). I stress myself out trying to keep up with all the chores as well as raising the children, which can be a handful. I've learnt that however stressed you are, when you see that innocent smile on your child's face appreciating you for being there for them, the hard work and stress levels disappear.

Before the birth of our first child, my husband and I bought our first house. The amount of budgeting and prep that we had to do made us realise what a great team we were. We've always wanted to run our own side business, but after my first son was born I felt the need to return to work to enable us to cope financially. Two years down the line, when I fell pregnant with my second son, our whole world changed. Even though I was assisting my husband with his publishing company and building our own business brand, we both felt that this was the right time for me to commit to being a mumpreneur.

Of course, being a mumpreneur is not without its challenges. And yes you may ask "Okay, now you've added an extra load onto doing all those household chores as well as running your own business". Yes, you're correct; however this is somewhat different for me. "Why?" Well first of all, if you're passionate about your work you will always find the time and never feel tired. Since I started my journey as a mumpreneur I have felt more energized and motivated. This attitude has also rubbed off on my children. I've noticed that children copy your every move and they look up to you as role models. By having a positive outlook on life and the determination to achieve the best you can, you will see a change in how your life will proceed. The added flexibility also enabled me to make a positive change to my lifestyle and the added bonus is that I still get to spend time with my children and be there for them as and when they need me.

Home life distractions do creep up when working at home, especially when you're fully focused on a project and you have a little person standing by your desk trying to get your attention. I've learnt that when you're running your own business and looking after your children, your time is much more your own and it's down to you to use it wisely.

I'm writing this book now to show all those inspirational mummies and even daddies out there that you can achieve anything that you set your mind to. All you have to do is be focused and motivated, to be the best you can be. Don't think someone else is doing it that way and they're doing a great job, so let's try that. You have to find the right method that works for you. Whichever and however you go about looking after your kids and business, you can do it your way which will be the right way.

Mumpreneurs out there, you're not alone. Let's make this present life a wonderful experience and a worthwhile one to look back upon. We can do it –Yes we can!

Emotional, yet the rock
Tired, but keeps going
Worried, but full of hope
Impatient, yet patient
Overwhelmed, but never quits
Amazing, even though doubted
Wonderful, even in the chaos
Life changer, every single day
~ Rachel Martin

MUMPRENEUR

A MULTITASKING WOMAN WHO CAN
BALANCE THE DEMANDS OF BEING AN
ENTREPRENEUR AND TAKE CARE OF THE
FAMILY AT THE SAME TIME

~CHAPTER 2~

10 KEY
JUGGLING
STRATEGIES

As mothers, we all struggle at one time or another in our lives with the juggling act of having to look after our children as well as working. There are so many balls that we have to keep up in the air! 24 hours in a day just sometimes isn't enough. It really is like a circus act, don't you agree?

Let's talk strategies. Now, we all know that there is no secret recipe to balancing motherhood and work life. Thousands of women have been doing it day in and day out and have become successful in their own respects. The known fact is that any one solution won't work for everyone. You need to find what works best for you.

Out of so many different strategies, the following ten are the top best tactics that I found useful in helping to balance the mumpreneur lifestyle. By putting these strategies into action you will instantly see the change it makes to your life.

1. **Get and Stay Organized** – Make sure everything is filed and in a place where you can access and find things easily. Being organized from the start will save you time and energy.

   Now this is the strategy I'm most good at. I always try to be super-organized, planning things in my head and getting things ready way in advance. Even when we go on trips or even to family events I always make sure we have two of everything, for example spare clothes, nappies, wipes, toys and even snacks for the journey just as precaution. You never know when you may get stuck in traffic or breakdown with two screaming children at the back of the car.

   But however organized you are, you're going to have to use this skill more than you ever have before. In terms of organization, do what works for you. For example, do a to-do list or use a whiteboard to highlight and plan ahead, but make sure you're efficient with your time.

2. **Plan Ahead** – Prepare your daily tasks and routines the night before so that you are all hands on deck the next morning. A to-do list is a great way to get started. I keep a diary, so every night I always jot down everything that needs to be done for the next day, and I tick these off as soon as I get each one done.

   Use your time wisely; get the meals prepared for the kids the night before so that you're not having to rush around, trying to prepare meals with two hungry children screaming to get your attention. Set aside some time to yourself to plan, even if it's only 15 minutes, just after you get the kids to bed to pre plan all the activities for the next day, refresh your mind, and most importantly, take a huge breath in and then release it out. Trust me, that will help you focus, relax and remove any mental stress. By focusing on breathing in then out, it's like meditating; it relieves you from the stresses and clears your mind. This will help energize you to be able to tackle the next day.

3. **Stay Focused** – Make sure you don't get distracted. The hardest thing for mums is that they get side tracked by their children or having to do the laundry or dishes. Make sure you have boundaries and set deadlines. Focus on one task at a time; don't let your mind stray from thinking of one task to another.

Be present in the task you're doing. I've had days when I'm looking after my boys and I'm on the phone doing my work at the same time. One day my eldest son came up to me and said 'Mummy NO phone'. He grabbed the phone from me and tossed it away. Instead of getting angry, I realized that my son wanted me to focus purely on him and not get distracted. So I decided to put my phone away and started dancing to songs with my boys. We literally spent an hour together, with me fully focusing my energy and thoughts on them. They seemed so happy and satisfied that mummy was putting her full energy and attention into them that once that hour was over and I had work to do, my kids were very well behaved and let me get on with my work for they knew they've had their 'me time' and it was now time for mummy to work.

I've learnt to realize that by focusing on the present moment I connect more with my sons and also with myself, and the more I appreciate and enjoy spending time with them without getting distracted by my thinking. So always remember to enjoy the moment as time and life are precious!

4. **Prioritize** – Always try and get the most important tasks out of the way first before touching anything else. Most importantly, you need to learn when to say 'no'. For me I'm the type of person who can never let anyone down. If I'm asked to do something, I always say 'Yes of course, that's fine'. It may be that by saying no I'm showing that I'm incapable of doing something but that's not the case. If you don't prioritize and force yourself to say 'no' you will become overworked and both your family and work will suffer.

5. **Work around your family** – Do your work while the kids are asleep by either staying up late or waking up before they do. Even try and get as much done while the kids have their naps during the day. Another method is to get the kids involved by allowing them to help you with the laundry, dishes and general cleaning. It will make them feel important and you'll get at least some things out of the way.

6. **Schedule a mummy day** – Take time out to just relax or even catch up with some friends. You will feel more energized after having some 'me' time.

   Even if you've planned everything to the smallest detail, you'll have days when your schedule has been disrupted and all the hard work put into planning your day just doesn't work out. Now that can be very stressful. In those circumstances you have to take a deep breath and let go and tell yourself that this is all part of life. Things won't always run smoothly and that's ok. There is always a lesson to be learnt in every challenge that needs to be overcome.

   Don't judge yourself or feel bad about taking time out for yourself. We're all human and we all need some 'me' time. After having kids, it can become daunting as you're so used to being around them 24/7, but by taking time out to just relax and refresh yourself you will be able to put more effort in and your children will see the happier you rather than the mummy who's always grumpy as she's stressed out with all the work overload.

7. **Ask for help** – Never be averse to asking for help. Everyone needs help now and then, so never be ashamed to rope in family and friends. Build your own support network. When my husband's at work, I always get the help from my parents and even my brother has been asked to help babysit while I take care of the house work. Even if you drop your kids off at their grandparents' house, you'll have at least a couple of hours to focus and get things done. Get your partner involved and then thank them for it.

   You may get along with your neighbors, and if they have kids then send yours over to their house for a couple of hours and vice versa. We all need to help one another. Trust me, the number of people who genuinely want to help is high, it's just that we're afraid or don't openly ask.

8. **Stay ahead of the game** – Set out the children's clothes for school the night before. Prepare the lunches and clean up so that the next morning will feel less hectic. You can even try and wake up early, have a shower and get a few minutes of exercise scheduled in. This will help you feel fresh and energized to start the day rather than sluggish.

9. **Look after yourself** – Make sure you take care of yourself by eating healthy and keeping up with exercise and getting enough sleep. You can get in some power naps during the day. You have to learn to accept the fact that there will never be enough time in the day to get everything done. You have to take care of yourself to be able to take care of your family, business and home. So mark what needs to be done on the calendar and move on.

10. **Perfection isn't a must** – Now your home doesn't always have to be spotless. You have kids, and visitors who come over will understand. Your priorities are your family and then your work. As long as the house is livable the kids won't care. All that will matter is that you're there for them! You have to come to terms with the fact that you can never be perfect and striving for perfection isn't a must. I know it's a difficult concept to master for all those over-achievers, as I'm a culprit of trying to be perfect and keep my household spotless if I want to feel like a super mum in the eyes of others. You just have to remember that perfection is an unattainable goal, especially in this situation. You have to take each day as it comes and trust me, however your house looks you're doing a great job!

The following will show how you could break down the 168 hours you have in a week to make you feel at your best.

You should try and fit in approximately 7 hours a week of 'me' time. This will help you unwind, feel chilled out and recharged.

Have roughly 8 hours a week for undertaking hobbies. This will lead to relaxation and fulfilment.

Your social life should also take 8 hours out of the week to give you the excitement, enjoyment and entertainment that you need in life.

Spend 10 hours per week with your friends. This will provide you with your daily dosage of laughter, fun and support.

22 hours should be spent on relationships. This will help make you feel loved, wanted and special.

Family brings understanding, closeness and belonging; therefore 25 hours should be spent around them.

Business gives you achievement, results and success, and thus most mumpreneurs spend roughly 39 hours per week on building it up.

Sleep should be your top priority, taking up approximately 49 hours per week. By having adequate amounts of sleep this will keep you energized, relaxed and rested. As you can see, a lot of emphasis has been put on sleep which is key. Make sure you get the adequate daily dosage.

Now, this is only a rough guide and the lengths of time do vary for each individual, so always draft your own unique schedule that works best for you.

Always think the best of yourself. By being motivated and self-driven, you will find out that you struggle less in balancing your work and family lifestyle. You will be less stressed and more carefree.

MUMPRENEUR TASK 1

Write down 5 things you struggle with and how you can juggle them. Set an approximate number of hours that you'll allocate to each one and try and stick by it.

Struggle 1:
....
....

Solution
....
....

Struggle 2:
....
....

Solution
....
....

Struggle 3:
....
....

Solution
....
....

Struggle 4:

....

....

Solution

....

....

Struggle 5:

....

....

Solution:

....

....

ALWAYS REMEMBER THAT THE METHOD IN
WHICH YOU USE TO COPE WITH THE STRUGGLES
DOESN'T MATTER. YOUR WAY WORKS BEST FOR
YOU AND YOUR FAMILY!
YOU'RE DOING A GREAT JOB!

~CHAPTER 3~

OVERCOMING THE CHALLENGES

Most work life balance conversations are usually between the 9 to 5 mums, or should I say the 5 to 9 mums versus the stay at home mums. The career orientated mums may find that they miss out on their children's milestones and have to give up on going to their children's school play as they have a board meeting to attend or other related work schedules. And there's the stay at home mums who get to go to all their children's school plays yet look longingly at their degree certificates hanging on the wall, thinking of what they could have become.

Now there is a third set of ladies who are on the rise, and these are our mumpreneurs. These are the mothers who multitask by looking after their business and their family at the same time. More women are now choosing to give up their careers and opt to stay at home and run their own businesses. The tempting advantages of having flexible hours, a potential to earn money, to be at home with your children for their core milestones, and to follow your dream of being your own boss can be some of the aspects that drive you to be a mumpreneur. However, taking on a home based business can have a fair share of challenges and is not always the 'easiest' path.

Now this can be a very daunting situation. As an entrepreneur, your clients may require your full attention but at the same time you have your toddler screaming for your attention and a baby who needs to be fed. Trust me, mothers, I know it all can get too overwhelming, but there are tactics that help with the process. In this chapter we will be looking into how we can overcome those challenges.

Some of the challenges that mumpreneurs face:

1. **Unannounced visitors**

   When you're a mumpreneur, you tend to get a lot more unannounced visitors as they expect you to be at home during the day, and they were just passing through the neighborhood and decided to drop by and have a catch up.

   If this does happen, then try and keep the visit short and explain to them that you have work to complete. I'm sure they'll understand, just don't say it in a harsh way.

2. **No scheduled closing time**

   For us ladies there never is a set time as to when we close for the day. Working from home tends to mean working around the clock.

   So prioritize and make sure you don't overwork yourself.

3. **Not enough time**

   The most common reason why most women nowadays tend to choose the life of a mumpreneur is that they think they will have a lot more time with their children and they will stop missing all those milestones. However, it is quite the contrary. As a mum, it's challenging enough looking after the children as well as doing all the housework let alone starting a business of your own from scratch. You will find that you are needing more hours in the day to enable you to juggle all three. You try to become super mum and all your needs tend to go out of the window. You start eating junk food as it's quick and easy to access. Give a call and takeaway will be there. So you begin to automatically prioritize your business rather than actually looking after your children.

So be kind to yourself. You have to remember you cannot make your business successful overnight.

4. Guilt

Guilt is a killer, and it tends to play a major part for mumpreneurs. Building up a business takes up time and energy. You really want to focus and get as much done as possible, but that can conflict with raising your family as you may feel that you're giving your children less time and attention. The whole point of being a mumpreneur gets forgotten and you're back to square one. This is the toughest challenge for most mumpreneurs.

The best way to overcome this challenge is to learn to give your 100% when you're with your children. Focus on them, and be present. Don't think about the tonnes of emails you have to respond to and the deadlines you have to meet. By being present you feel less guilt and more satisfied with yourself. Always be open-minded and have realistic expectations. At the end of the day you have to be proud of your achievements. You're running your own business as well as raising wonderful children.

5. Balanced Lifestyle

Getting the work-home life balance is always quite tricky. It's not only the mumpreneurs that struggle, the working mums do too.

Now this may seem quite obvious, but make a structured plan. Make a conscious effort to schedule in some non-negotiable family time. By doing so you can't back out, and make the effort to spend quality time with your family. Eating together is a great way to bond and it's a good time for you to listen to your children and for them to talk openly to you.

The key to overcoming all challenges is
TIME MANAGEMENT!

By managing your time effectively you'll find that you're less stressed and run down. It has been proven that people work best first thing in the morning, so try and set a solid block in the morning free to get things done. That way you can spend quality time with your family in the evening.

Have planners where you set times in which tasks need to be done. Keep an hour or so free on Sunday to plan ahead for the week, such as what lunch and dinners to prepare. That way you're all set and not having to think about what to do next. This will even help with the shopping list.

Make sure you get fresh air by going for a brisk 15 minute walk. This will help rejuvenate your mind and you will be ready to focus.

Reduce procrastination and discipline yourself. This will help you to avoid doing unnecessary tasks.

Make sure you make time for your children when they need you. You must not forget that you are doing this for them and they should take utmost importance in your life. The biggest mistake I used to make was using my phone when spending time with my kids. If you're on the phone using social media or checking your emails, your children won't get 100% of your attention so they get frustrated and act up. The point of spending time with them is ruined and loses all purpose. Therefore avoid technology and social media. Take your kids out to have some fun like the good old days when technology didn't exist. The kids will definitely appreciate your full focus and attention on them and learn to understand that you love them unconditionally.

Remember to be motivated by and mindful of your children.

MUMPRENEUR TASK 2

Write down 5 challenges you face and how you can overcome them.

Struggle 1:
....
....

Solution
....
....

Struggle 2:
....
....

Solution
....
....

Struggle 3:
....
....

Solution
....
....

Struggle 4:
....
....

Solution
....
....

Struggle 5:

....

....

Solution:

....

....

ALWAYS REMEMBER THAT THE METHOD IN
WHICH YOU USE TO COPE WITH THE
CHALLENGES DOESN'T MATTER. YOUR WAY
WORKS BEST FOR YOU AND YOUR FAMILY!
YOU'RE DOING A GREAT JOB!

~CHAPTER 4 ~

SELFCARE

Make self-care a priority! It can be a daunting feeling putting yourself as priority when you have to care for your children as they always tend to take top priority. The key thing to remember is that you are number one, because if you don't take care of yourself you won't be able to take care of your children. There are ways you can feel healthy, look great and live a joyful life at the same time, as well as juggle a family with a career.

The key is to balance life with a healthy diet by making purposeful choices to rejuvenate the body, mind and soul.

You must be thinking, 'Sure it's easy for you to say but definitely hard to do'. Well, yes you're right it is hard, but without hard work you won't achieve anything.

I've always thought that I would set an example to my kids and make sure I eat healthy and put in a lot of exercise, but quite the contrary: I ended up eating junk food where and when I could fit in snacking time and I began to put on tremendous weight.

Therefore make sure you set an intention to look after yourself the moment you become a mother and commit to caring for your child(ren). As most mums know, when breastfeeding, you need to have a nutritional diet for your baby to benefit from the mother's milk, so we all tend to make the effort to eat more healthily. But once we stop, sneaky habits of eating junk may creep in. Junk food will mentally slow you down and make you feel sluggish. By eating healthier you will feel refreshed and energetic.

To get you started, make sure you have a self-care mindset. Here are some tips on caring for yourself and making 'YOU' the priority.

1. Exercise

Make sure you include at least 15 minutes of exercise in your daily routine every day. It doesn't have to mean you have to go to the gym to work out; I personally think doing the housework is exercise. There are many mums out there who exercise with their children. You can have a dance marathon, run up and down your stairs a hundred times (ok, maybe slight exaggeration, but you get what I'm trying to say) or even go to the little toddler gyms where you can bring your children. The positive side to getting the kids involved is that the more you tire them out the better they'll sleep, which will give you some extra 'me time'.

Here are some quick and easy 15 minute exercises that you can simply do at home (these workouts have been taken from an article written by Larysa Didio).

Chair Dip

Using a sturdy chair, place your hands next to your hip whilst sitting down. Slowly slide your bottom off the chair and keep going down until your elbows are at a 90 degrees angle. Make sure to keep your back close to the chair. Then push yourself back into the seating position. Repeat this 10 times.

Chair Squats

Stand facing away from the chair with both your arms in front of you. Place your feet hip-distance apart. Bend your knees and slowly place your bottom on the chair but don't sit down. Make sure to keep your weight on your heels and your knees should at all times be positioned above your toes. Repeat 10 times.

Butterfly Abs

With the palm of your feet together and your hands on you head, lie down on your back. Face your elbows outwards. Lift your chest and shoulders up slowly and release back down. This will tighten your abs. Repeat 10 times.

Oblique Crunches

While lying on your back, bend your knees. Then cross the left ankle on top of your right knee and place your right hand on your head with the elbow facing out and your left arm relaxed on the floor. Then lift your right shoulder towards your left knee and then release slowly. Repeat this 10 times and then switch sides.

Modified Push-ups

Lie facing down on all fours. Make sure your knees are placed together and place your hands slightly wider than your chest. Your head, neck, back and bottom should aligned. Bend your elbows slowly whilst keeping your abs tight and lower your chest towards the floor. Repeat these pushups 10 times.

Standing Hip Extension

Stand behind the chair with your feet placed hip-distance apart. Extend your left leg and place your weight on your right foot. Lift and lower your left foot simultaneously squeezing your bottom. The chair should be used to keep your balance. Repeat 10 times then switch legs.

Step Ups

You can do this exercise at the bottom of your stairs. Put your right foot on the stair and step onto the stair with your left foot. Then step off the stair with the left foot followed by the right. Make sure to keep your chest lifted. Repeat this 10 times then complete another ten starting off with the left foot. You can start using weights once you get stronger.

2. Healthy diet

It's always a natural tendency for mothers to put their child(ren) first. Make sure they're fully fed before they even think about what they're going to have, but it is also a necessity that you get the right balance of nutritional food to keep your energy levels high. All you need to do is to put a few minutes aside to plan what you'll be having each day of the week so that you can make sure your fridge is stocked with everything you require to make an easy, quick, healthy meal.

Here are some super foods for mothers: salmon, eggs, brown rice, blueberries, spinach, oatmeal, almonds and milk.

Quick and healthy energy boosting snacks: bananas, veggies and hummus, Greek yoghurt and berries, nuts, cheese and crackers, no bake energy bites.

3. Meditation

Meditation will help relieve you from any stress. When you meditate you will forget about everything and focus purely on your breathing. By doing so it will help clear your mind and make you feel a lot more relaxed to take on the challenges of being a mumpreneur.

4. Prioritize sleep

Make sure you get the daily dosage of sleep that's required. By doing so you won't feel so run down. Power naps are a great way to refresh your brain, but with power naps you have to ensure that you don't drift off thinking about everything you have to do that day. Fully focus on being relaxed. Set your alarm to wake you up.

AMAZING
LOVELY
INTELLIGIENT
HAPPY
BEAUTIFUL
MARVELLOUS

~CHAPTER 5~

S.C.A.M.P.E.R

(The creative brainstorming tool)

The S.C.A.M.P.E.R method is a very creative brainstorming tool that I researched. It is a very effective tool that I wanted to share with my readers. It is not something that I've come up with but definitely something that I found useful being a mumpreneur, and I hope this helps you too. I've adapted the tool to fit our mumpreneur needs.

This tool was developed by a gentleman called Robert Eberle who used a list by the marketing guru of brainstorming, Alex Osborn, to develop the creative brainstorming tool, S.C.A.M.P.E.R. The word is an acronym which helps trigger ideas by using seven active verbs.

In this chapter I will be showing you how you can use this creative brainstorming tool in your everyday life as a mumpreneur and how it could be implemented.

These are the seven active words you need to focus on. The mnemonic stands for:

S = Substitute
C = Combine
A = Adapt
M = Modify
P = Put to other use
E = Eliminate
R = Rearrange

<u>S</u>ubstitute

Are there ways you can substitute your current method you work with and use a better method that will speed up your process? For example my eldest son had started nursery and I always used to go and pick him up, which took an hour of my time as I had to get the little one ready and fed. Getting the buggy in and out of the car was a mission; therefore I got my dad to help out with picking up my son, so that saved me some extra time to be more productive in doing something else.

Combine

Think of the activities and tasks that you can combine to help you save time. For example, when I'm cooking I also listen to inspiring YouTube videos to keep on track with my work. I also get the kids to help out with the hoovering and I even dance with them to keep them occupied, but that's also part of my exercise regime.

Adapt

Get ideas and tips from other mumpreneurs and try and adopt them into your daily schedule to make you more efficient. Choose the ones that work best for you and your family.

Modify

Jot down tasks that you can modify in your day to day activities to minimize the time you spend on certain activities. You can change the number of times you do your laundry to say set days of only twice a week.

Put to other use

Get a team on board. Delegate your tasks so that you're not overworked. You can train other people to do certain tasks to allow you to spend more time with the family.

My husband and I work well together as a team. He normally makes the teas for us and the milk for the kids in the morning and I do the ironing. You have to see what you're best at and use it to speed up the process.

Eliminate

Think about the things you could eliminate from your life. I found by cutting out negative people from my life I was made to feel more positive about life. Getting to know like-minded individuals helped me to be motivated and energized to take on any task. Take each day as it comes and make the most of every waking hour.

Rearrange

Think about how you can rearrange your day to day activities to make it more family and work friendly. For example instead of making the lunches first thing in the morning, you can get them ready the night before so it frees up more time, leaving you less stressed the next day. If you start the day stress free and relaxed, chances are your happy mood will make the day a more positive one.

~CHAPTER 6~

MINDSET
(Physical & Mental Development)

Being a mumpreneur is not just about excelling in your career and family life, but more about mindset and lifestyle.
You have to remember, if you do nothing then nothing happens. To get things done you need to set your mind to it. Don't procrastinate and just do it!

Set realistic tasks and delegate the tasks that don't fall under your expertise. You shouldn't be ashamed to ask for help. My mother usually helps with cooking as I'm yet to master certain traditional recipes.

Make sure that you spend your time as productively as possible. Schedule in exercise to make sure you rejuvenate your physical and mental appearance. The healthier you are the more energy you'll have to undertake your daily tasks.

Your physical, mental and emotional wellbeing should be top priority. This will help you remain balanced in everything you do. The most powerful muscle is your mind, so make sure you keep it active by continuously learning through reading books and even taking time out to meditate which will refresh your mind and soul.

Avoid worrying about perfection by getting started. While you're trying your best to get everything perfect, there's someone out there who has started. Action makes the magic happen, so don't wait for miracles to happen. You make it happen! Build yourself a team who will help you through the process, and surround yourself with likeminded individuals. By inspiring and motivating one another you can reach high expectations.

If you feel pressure don't take it as a negative thing. Look on the brighter side and appreciate that it is an opportunity for you to grow and develop yourself. Women are always feeling pressured to be super women but remember, you have to set your own standards and block out any negativity and pressure that's not really relevant to you.

Don't over-think the work-life balance, try to think of it as work-life integration. Do what works best for you. It may be that you work best in the early hours of the morning or late at night. Just work yourself around your family and everything else will fall into place.

Be strong, be brave, be flexible and be present!

Always remember to trust in your full potential. Surround yourself with likeminded and positive people to help drive you forward. Don't dwell on your past performance; focus on the present and aim to achieve your goals. As mothers, we often forget to appreciate the things we do and feel blessed and grateful for everything we have and have already achieved. .

Surround yourself with positivity. Avoid talking to people who bring you down as it's not worth being in a negative aura. Listen to motivational speakers who will guide you in driving forward and help you focus on your goals.

Believe in yourself, be confident and thrive for the best you can be! Stop thinking negative thoughts because the way you think will affect your behavior. You are capable of balancing your family, work and home life. Start acknowledging how brilliant you are and how much you have accomplished. Come on, it's not easy giving birth to such adorable kids. They're one of your biggest life achievements. So start believing in your full potential.

Have a clear definition of what you want and this will make it more attainable. Focus on dreaming big and then find a way to make it work for you.

If you're unhappy where you are then you're in the wrong place. Get into a relationship with yourself. Learn to understand your true self by asking yourself some honest questions and follow through with the answers. Be grateful for everything you have. Keep a gratitude journal and write down something you're grateful for every day, and you will be surprised by how many you can think of.

By changing your mindset today you can look forward to a lifetime of success in everything you do.

~CHAPTER 7~

BECOMING AN ENTREPRENEURIAL MUM

My vision of being an entrepreneurial mum, a "mumpreneur", was being able to be flexible with your time, creating your own schedule and most importantly being able to look after and share the milestones of my children. I have seen so many stay-at-home mums and even working mums who have left their 9 to 5 jobs to become entrepreneurs and set up their own home-based business. Now, what most people forget is that the qualities of an entrepreneur are similar to being a mum. Raising children and being your own boss comes with its fair share of challenges. In both scenarios you need to be organized, task-orientated and efficient with your time.

As mothers, I believe we have the essential skills required of an entrepreneur. The five top skills are: working under pressure, negotiation skills, creativity and the ability to crowdsource, putting your ego aside and weighing your pros and cons.

If you've ever thought motherhood will hold you back from being an entrepreneur and starting your own venture, then think again.

If you're thinking of becoming an entrepreneurial mum, then make sure you can answer the following question.

What are you passionate about?

Once you've found the answer the rest is simple. When you're trying to balance work and kids at home, the passion and drive for your business will propel you forward to succeed.

As a mumpreneur, my tip to you will be **INVEST** in **YOURSELF**. Make sure you're constantly learning. Enroll in courses and even have a coach to guide you. You must remember that you're not alone. Don't stress yourself out trying to find solutions. Think innovatively and practically. Throughout our childhood, from school to university, we have our teachers' guidance, and when we start work we have training and induction days. Therefore as self-employed mums we need to continue to learn by either having a mentor or even through online courses.

Make sure you set personal and business goals. By setting goals you are on the right path to fulfilling them quicker. Read them aloud every day and this will motivate you to achieve them.

What are your goals?

Do your research by reading up on other successful mumpreneurs. Doing this helped me to be driven and focus on my goals. Surrounding yourself with like-minded individuals will also play a part in you becoming a successful entrepreneur and may inspire your own business idea.

All entrepreneurs are good at having their own business plan, but have you considered having your own personal plan? A plan that relates to you on a long-term basis? Be realistic. Take into consideration how your time will change as your children get older. I like to write things down, such as doing the laundry and even pointless things like calling a friend, just so that I can tick them off my list. It gives such gratification when I do so.

Having a home-based business doesn't have to mean that you stay in your pajamas all day. As a mumpreneur I've learnt with time that the phrase "dress to impress" does play a key role in making me feel better about myself. Some mums might find this quite controversial, but by dressing how you would if you were going out and physically meeting people will make you work more productively. I've found by doing so I'm more motivated and focused. I really do encourage you to try it for one week and see how your attitude and mood changes and makes you feel.

Develop your own daily schedule. For example, read your emails while the kids are in bed, make sure dinner time is spent focusing entirely on your family and return to doing your work whilst the kids are in nursery or school. If you have children under the age of two then try managing your time around nap times by working in short bursts and resting during feeds.

Make sure you separate your work from looking after your children. There are bound to be times when both worlds will collide. But by keeping them separate you will be giving your full focus to the task at hand. Your productivity will increase and you will begin to enjoy all the positives of being a mother rather than stressing over running a business. Don't lose focus on why you became a mumpreneur in the first place!

As a mumpreneur don't forget to get your children engaged in your activities. It's always best to start them young. Never be afraid to get your children involved. Give them work-related tasks such as filing and even encourage them to come up with their own ideas. You'll be surprised as to how children think. Try it! Children who are exposed to the entrepreneurial world will have a better understanding of hard work and have the determination and to thrive and succeed.

Organization and time management are both key qualities of both a mother and an entrepreneur. If these qualities are not your strength then make sure to build up and learn to commit to these qualities. With the amount of technology in this day and age, there are no excuses. You can update your calendars and even make to-do lists on your phone while you're on the go or even whilst waiting to pick up your kids. Make use of every spare second. There will be no regrets in life, just lessons learnt.

In this chapter I have put together organizers for you to help with your daily tasks. You can download your own FREE pintables at www.universallearningacademy.com.

"For every minute spent organizing, an hour is earned."

- **Benjamin Franklin**

MEAL PLANNER

WEEKLY MENU

DATE/MONTH/YEAR

UNIVERSAL LEARNING ACADEMY

MONDAY

BREAKFAST

LUNCH

DINNER

TUESDAY

BREAKFAST

LUNCH

DINNER

WEDNESDAY

BREAKFAST

LUNCH

DINNER

THURSDAY

BREAKFAST

LUNCH

DINNER

FRIDAY

BREAKFAST

LUNCH

DINNER

HEALTHY EATING MENU PLAN

MON
B: ....
L: ....
D: ....

TUES
B: ....
L: ....
D: ....

WED
B: ....
L: ....
D: ....

THURS
B: ....
L: ....
D: ....

FRI
B: ....
L: ....
D: ....

SAT
B: ....
L: ....
D: ....

SUN
B: ....
L: ....
D: ....

UNIVERSAL LEARNING ACADEMY

to do this week

MONTH: / WEEK:

SUN

MON

TUES

WED

THURS

FRI

SAT

NOTES

DON'T FORGET

_____

_____

_____

_____

_____

UNIVERSAL LEARNING ACADEMY

WEEKLY MENU

MONDAY
Breakfast...
Lunch...
Dinner..

TUESDAY
Breakfast...
Lunch...
Dinner..

WEDNESDAY
Breakfast...
Lunch...
Dinner..

THURSDAY
Breakfast...
Lunch...
Dinner..

FRIDAY
Breakfast...
Lunch...
Dinner..

SATURDAY
Breakfast...
Lunch...
Dinner..

SUNDAY
Breakfast...
Lunch...
Dinner..

MUMPRENEURS
HOW TO JUGGLE THE STRUGGLE

SHOPPING LIST

- [ ] ....
- [ ] ....
- [ ] ....
- [ ] ....
- [ ] ....
- [ ] ....
- [ ] ....
- [ ] ....
- [ ] ....
- [ ] ....
- [ ] ....
- [ ] ....
- [ ] ....
- [ ] ....
- [ ] ....
- [ ] ....
- [ ] ....
- [ ] ....
- [ ] ....
- [ ] ....
- [ ] ....
- [ ] ....

WEEKLY SCHEDULE

	Monday	Tuesday	Wednesday	Thursday	Friday	Saturday	Sunday
6AM	Daily prep	Daily prep	Daily prep	Daily prep	Daily prep	Daily prep	Daily prep
7AM	Breakfast	Breakfast	Breakfast	Breakfast	Breakfast	Breakfast	Breakfast
8AM	Nursery drop-offs	Nursery drop-offs	Nursery drop-offs	Nursery drop-offs	Nursery drop-offs	Prepare for the next day	Prepare for the next day
9AM	Work	Work	Work	Order Groceries	Work	Family Time	Family Time
10AM	Work	Work	Work	Work	Work	Family Time	Family Time
11AM	Nursery Pick ups	Nursery Pick ups	Nursery Pick ups	Nursery Pick ups	Nursery Pick ups	Family Time	Family Time
12PM	Lunch	Lunch	Lunch	Lunch	Lunch	Lunch	Lunch
1PM	Work	Work	Work	Work	Work	Work	Work
2PM	Work	Work	Work	Work	Work	Work	Work
3PM	Work	Work	Work	Work	Work	Work	Work
4PM	Family time	Family time	Family time	Family time	Family time	Family time	Family time
5PM	Dinner	Dinner	Dinner	Dinner	Dinner	Dinner	Dinner
6PM	Cleaning	Cleaning	Cleaning	Cleaning	Cleaning	Family time	Family time
7PM	Bedtime routine for the kids	Bedtime routine for the kids	Bedtime routine for the kids	Bedtime routine for the kids	Bedtime routine for the kids	Bedtime routine for the kids	Bedtime routine for the kids
8PM	Self-care	Self-care	Self-care	Self-care	Self-care	Social/Family time	Social/Family time
9PM	Prepare for the next day	Prepare for the next day	Prepare for the next day	Prepare for the next day	Prepare for the next day	Social/Family time	Social/Family time
10PM	Work	Work	Work	Work	Work	Social/Family time	Social/Family time
11PM	Work	Work	Work	Work	Work	Work	Work

MUMPRENEURS
How to Juggle the Struggle

✳✳✳✳✳✳✳✳✳✳✳✳✳✳✳✳✳✳✳✳✳✳✳✳

~CHAPTER 8~

INSPIRATIONAL MUMPRENEURS THE INSIDE STORY

In this chapter we will be looking into the lives of nine inspirational mothers and their view points – the inside story. I was intrigued to see the variety of mums out there and the different ways in which they tackled motherhood along with work. All these women have unique stories and different methods of coping with everyday work and family life balance. They ALL are true INSPIRATIONS in their own respectful ways.

The following was asked of them:

- Brief background about themselves
- How they cope with the struggles of being a working mum
- Useful tips and tools to overcome the struggles

It was lovely to hear back from so many wonderful and inspirational mumpreneurs who were willing to take time out of their busy schedules to contribute to this chapter. I am truly grateful, and I'm sure these stories will bring great inspiration and motivation to all you readers.

"If you set your mind to it, nothing is impossible!"

Sabrina Ben Salmi
(BSc mother of Fantastic 5, Author, Founder of 21 Day SHIFT HAPPENS & Dreaming Big Together, Director of Harris Invictus, & Business/Personal Development Consultant)

BYA Mother of The Year Award Winner Sabrina Ben Salmi is a proud mother of 5 entrepreneurial children from 4yrs old to 17yrs old, who she referees to as her Fantastic 5. Sabrina is a multi-award winning author, business and personal development coach/mentor, a founding director of Ofsted outstanding Harris Invictus Academy (Secondary School), former radio show host, and public speaker. Founder of Dreaming Big Together and 21 Day Shift Happens. Mrs Sabrina Ben Salmi BSc is here to empower you to plant the seed so that you and your family can learn to Dream Big Together via a variety of products and services that aim to assist you and your loved ones to create a brighter future. Sabrina has been featured in the media via radio, TV, newspapers, magazines, etc. to name a few: Channel 4 Secret Millionaire, BBC London News, LBC Radio, BBC Radio, Fabulous Magazine.

"It's about time that we stop giving our children indefinite time to remain on the streets and empower them to plant the seed for a brighter tomorrow."

As a mother of 5 it's absolutely paramount that I schedule my daily activities in advance. This enables me to complete daily responsibilities.

As a stay at home mother of 5, I am often faced with a host of unexpected issuesthat often results in me having to cancel prior plans due to having to adhere to family responsibilities. When this takes place, first I remind myself to become conscious of my breath and then take three deep breaths, because it is human nature to trigger hollow breathing during stressful periods. I then remind myself that I am doing my best and that I love my precious family beyond words, and then I (((SMILE))). I also ask for help and advice when needed; after all, it takes a village to raise a child.

As a mother it's easy to fill your day with 101 things to adhere to for your precious family, friends and clients.

However this will merely lead to serious physical and emotional repercussion as time goose on. When I'm working with clients on constantly remind them of the importance of building a team and taking time out to focus on your needs by asking for help, leveraging support and advice and also taking time out to simply reconnect with yourself (depending on how busy your lifestyle is). It doesn't matter how short the time is, what matters most is consistency. For example, a minimum of 10-15 mins daily to meditate, read, go for a walk or simply list that which you are grateful for can trigger a huge shift.

Repeating an affirmation could also leave you feeling reenergised

-"Wouldn't it be nice if...?"
- "I apologise to myself and others, I forgive myself and others, I appreciate myself and other, I love myself and others."
- "All of life supports me upon an adult basis."
- "My health is my wealth."
- "When I choose to care for myself and ask for help when needed, I am then able to show up as the best version of myself for myself and others."
- "Who do I need to become in order to be, do and manifest my dreams and aspirations?"

"Sabrina Ben Salmi will help you create the life you deserve. Writer of Lone Parenthood and mother of Lashai and Trey Sean who wrote Kidz That Dream Big, Sabrina Ben Salmi helps you to grow in your business and your relationships."

www.sabrinabensalmi.com
www.10secondstochildgenius.co.uk
Twitter: @wwwtmspporg
YouTube: Sabrina Ben Salmi
Facebook: Sabrina Ben Salmi
Facebook: 21 Days SHIFT HAPPENS

Arabi Kartheepan
(BSc Mathematics and Physics with Astrophysics PGCE Science Education)

I am a secondary school Physics teacher and a mother of two beautiful daughters. My eldest daughter is 4 years old and has started reception. My second daughter is 5 months old.
Managing motherhood and work life is a constantly evolving relationship. Just when you think you've got a good relationship, changes occur along the way and you have to readjust the relationship.

Being a teacher compels you to bring school work home, as there is never enough school hours to do your work. When I bring school work home, my work is never really finished! It is inevitable; there is always something left to do. I struggled to find a work life balance after returning from my maternity leave. I resumed my school work after coming home by working throughout the evening continuously till midnight and working on the weekends too. My husband and daughter, who was 1 at the time, barely had time to interact with me. I felt really guilty and horrible for not being a good wife or mother.

Solution: I found short cuts to ensure I limited bringing school work home. The moment I had at least 5 minutes to spare during the school day, I would use that to plan my lessons, prepare my class, mark books, respond to emails, etc. I maximised my hours at work so that all my preparation and marking were done before I left. I used up a few sacrificial Sundays to prepare for the upcoming weeks to free up my evenings and weekends. By doing this, I have had time to spend with my family and to enjoy days out on the weekends.

I dread going out with the whole family if it is unexpected and not planned. It can ruin my day if I have forgotten to stock up the bag with a spare change of clothes or a spare nappy. It's a disaster when forgetting to buy a card and a gift, which adds an extra 30 minutes to the ETA to the party!

> ➤ The planning solution: I created my own personalised calendar mapped out for the entire year ahead. I have this placed on our central hub, the kitchen notice board. I add the following: events, birthdays, family days out, holidays, husband's night out, meet ups with friends and work commitments. By doing this, it allows me and my husband to plan around and prepare ourselves and the children. We plan our days out carefully so that we aren't overworked during the week and weekend.

> ➤ For birthdays and events, the big mission is to get myself, my husband and my daughter's outfits ready. It's a daunting task if it's left to the last minute of the day.

> ➤ The outfit solution: I plan ahead (weeks or even months before) and have all of our outfits stitched or bought ahead of the event and laid out the night before with all the matching accessories. I plan my daughter's bathing schedule so it falls on the night before, as I've had the experience of bathing my daughters on the day of going out and they always end up catching a cold! I ensure that my bag is packed to take with me, which includes spare clothes for each of my daughters, Pampers, wipes, and spare clothes for myself to change into because I end up completely drained by the end of the event.

> ➤ The gift and card solution: Birthday cards for the family and extended family are bought in advance for

the entire year. I stock up on spare birthday, thank you, wedding and blank cards for unexpected events that pop up on our calendar.

I order online or plan a trip to the shopping mall to buy gifts weeks ahead, or sometimes, months ahead. Especially when it's Christmas, my presents are bought and wrapped a month before Christmas!

The holiday solution: I am a spreadsheet freak. I pretty much use it to plan everything! It's the best thing to plan my personal family holidays.

I created a tab for the following:

- Holiday budget - very good to keep track on the financing and pushes you to find good deals
- Holiday checklist – I have made a list for myself, husband and my 2 daughters on what I need to pack to take with us. I reuse the checklist for the following holiday and make a few changes.
- List of places to visit – I research if the attraction has baby changing facilities, wheelchair access and is buggy friendly.

There are times when I feel completely overwhelmed by being a working mother. I didn't have the luxury of family help when my eldest was 2 and had to find ways to manage my family independently since then. I look back to see what I have achieved with my family and realise that "I am doing the best I possibly can in the given situation".

Useful Tools:

- I subscribed to emails from https://www.babycentre.co.uk/ since I was pregnant with my first child. This has been a lifesaving parenting tool which keeps me updated on milestones, things to expect and parenting tips.

Rushani Mahendran
(Founder and Author of The 15 Minute Startup)

Coming from a strong corporate background I have always valued having strong systems and processes in place. After having my daughter 3 years ago, I decided I needed to find work that was more flexible that would still utilise my experience and skillset without having to sacrifice time with my family. That's when I started my entrepreneurial journey, and while it has been extremely exciting and fulfilling it also came with a steep learning curve and lots of challenges.

My biggest challenge was the complete lack of systems and processes in the online world, and throw trying to work around children into the mix and in the beginning I felt like I was surrounded by complete chaos. However, once you find your way around and start to get to grips with the mindset required to become an entrepreneur, things start to calm down and you can find a way to put your own systems in place.

As a mumpreneur I know that I'm not going to have long before I might be interrupted because my children need me, and rather than get frustrated that I can't focus or have enough time to concentrate on my work, I've learned to change my approach instead.

I never plan to do more than 15 minutes of work at a time. That way I know I can reasonably get one thing done and tick it off my list before I get interrupted, because nothing frustrates me more than leaving something unfinished. I then have 4-5 15 minute activities planned for each day which is a reasonable amount of progress.

15 minutes might not sound like a lot, but when you know that's all you have you'll be surprised at how super focused

you become and your productivity shoots through the roof. Over time I've gotten faster at getting things done, which means I can now get more done in 15 minutes than I've ever been able to.

And that is why I started the15minutestartup.com. As a mumpreneur there is no time to be wasted learning long, complex processes that to be honest are extremely unproductive and where it could take months before you see any results in your business. While it does take time and consistent effort to build a business, I do still make sure I am finding the best business models that don't take too much time to get started.

On my blog you'll find business ideas that you can start in 15 minutes or less and my best hacks for cutting down the time it takes to complete they key activities in your business. Things only take as long as we allow them to, so the key is to cut down on procrastinating and get laser focused so that you can use even the little time you do have as a mumpreneur effectively.

Fiona Seigneur
(Founder of Seigneur Strategies)

Imagine leaving a country where the sun is shining and it's 35 degrees only to land in another country where it's freezing, and while there was sun where you left there is now snow! OMG the amount of times I heard this story from my late dad! My parents were Mauritian and immigrated to England when they were in their twenties.

Little did I know then years later we'd be doing the same thing, i.e. immigrating to another country. I was born in England, but my family and I immigrated to Australia when I was a young child. My plan after secondary school was to return to England for a working holiday. However, as with all goals, things may not always happen in a straight line or within the time you planned for.

In my case, instead of travelling when I started work, I found myself working and dating and staying in the same country! Dating then led me to a man that at that time I thought connected with me on all levels. Along the journey, we got married and had 2 beautiful boys, only to find years later that it came time for us to go our own way and soon a divorce ensued. Since that time, I've been a single mother for over 10 years.

Have you ever struggled with something so much and felt inadequate for doing so? At that time, I certainly did. I loved working full time and yet I was raising my youngest son, who has Asperger Syndrome, in the same way I was raised: quite strictly. This would sometimes cause concern to the school and I would get phone calls from the school re: my youngest boy. It became quite apparent that, although he and my other son handled the stress of moving quite well, I had underestimated what a difference the Australian and English culture was to be for me in the first few years.

As my boys grew older this challenge only grew more, and it started to become obvious that the other parents and their children were happy to accept my eldest to have play days and sleepovers, however my younger boy was quite a loner. So I compensated by becoming his best friend.

The emotional role of being a mother and your son's best friend while holding down a full time and often demanding job took its toll and after a while I found myself totally burnt out and suffering from both physical and emotional exhaustion.]I ignored what I felt and told no one, telling myself I'd get through this. However, I didn't realise how much worse ignoring what I felt was for me.

So for anyone reading this who is suffering silently, you don't have to. Things can get better: reach out and speak to someone you trust about how you are feeling.

In the end, me keeping how I felt inside affected my corporate career and eventually my health.

During the time of my career, I would drop my boys off with a neighbour who was also a registered child minder, and in the afternoons I was so grateful for an after school club where they would stay every day after school. However as my job became more demanding and I was needing to put in more hours, I would find myself rushing through traffic to pick up the boys who were often the last ones there and then end up having to pay extra. I hated seeing the sullen looks on the faces of the after school care team, and it wasn't long before things deteriorated even more and eventually I fell into depression.

Now I see that was a turning point for my life. One can only drive a car so long on no fuel. I returned to Australia to recover and recharge, although it killed me to have to leave my children. Thankfully, it wasn't long until I reunited with them again.

My return was a huge challenge for all of us as I wasn't the same ambitious woman they and I knew. However I continued to work on my recovery and pick up relatively stress-free jobs to make ends meet; sometimes I would work 2-3 jobs in a day. It wasn't easy, but I'm grateful it gave me the flexibility to look after my children and their wellbeing as I kept working on myself.

I had always planned that by the time my boys were the age they are now, I would be working in a high level corporate position again.

As said earlier, life isn't always a straight line, and after recognising all those years of pushing myself relentlessly, worrying about things I couldn't change and feeling stagnant meant I needed to accept that all things were possible but it was going to take time to retrain my brain again. I began to plan how I could use what I went through to help others, and Seigneur Strategies was born.

At Seigneur Strategies we help young females aged 17-25 to recover from early depression and stress using natural remedies to work alongside current GP care plans with access to a team of great professionals, most who have been along a similar journey as a teen or young adult.

Working as an entrepreneurial mum now means I can be home when the kids are home and organise my day around my clients- which for me has made all the positive difference in so many ways. And now in the last year I can say I've been blessed with a strong network of support and kinship from a few ladies I'm blessed to know, because it can be quite isolating.

So in conclusion, if you are a single mum, entrepreneur woman or just a woman seeking to improve your situation, don't keep to yourself. Reach out to others and together we can all make a positive difference. Thank you for the opportunity to share with you.

Prasanthika Mihirani
(Founder of SwissGraphics)

I'm a 34 year old mum from Sri Lanka, who has two little daughters and a lovely husband. My husband is a businessmen and I worked as a personal secretary in a leading bank network in Sri Lanka years ago. After marriage, I decided to resign and develop our own business with my husband.

My daughters are just 5 years and 2 1/2 now. I was a working woman till my marriage and had to leave my job and then became a stay-at-home mother. But I joined my husband's business till my elder daughter's birth. As an Asian woman we have more responsibilities in our family, so I found a better way to use my skills and look after my kids at the same time. As a result, now I'm a successful freelancer and a lovely mum to my daughters. Not only that, I am a proud lady who gives a strong backup to our family income.

It is not simple to look after kids and work as a freelancer at the same time, especially since my daughters are still too small and they can't do anything without help. They also need their parents' attention at this age. So I should manage my time schedule and my day and keep balancing these two roles. Also, personally we both don't like to leave our kids with babysitters or daycare, so all the daily tasks of caring for my daughters such as cleaning, feeding, etc. are done by myself. I enjoy my time with them and it's a very common thing in our country.

Sometimes I wish I could have more hours in the day to complete all these things (lol). As a designer I should have a calm and peaceful environment to do something new. But with my kids, that is usually just a dream. So I found a way to balance home and job. I used to work at night and when they were sleeping and then I could spend the whole day with my lovely daughters.

As our business is related to computer technology, I wanted to use and improve my skills according to the business. So now I have 10+ years of experience in the graphic designing field and 4 years of experience as a freelancer. My husband and I are both graphic designers and he is also a computer technician. Here is the link to our Facebook page: https://www.facebook.com/swissGraphics/

Dedication is the most important tip I would give to being a good mumpreneur. We may not get a proper sleep, have time to eat, or even time to think. But that's not a reason to fail. I never get stressed or feel the tension. If we try we can make time for our needs. And I always trust myself. Fortunately, I have a very good, understanding husband to help with all my work.

Trust yourself and be dedicated to fulfill your future dreams!

Victoria Fellowes
(Founder of StrideForth, Professional qualms: CPC, ELI-MP)

I am a career specialist (coach, consultant, mentor and teacher) who works with people to master their careers and accelerate upwards and outwards quickly, practically and sustainably. My clients enjoy the benefits of quick results and of having a strong, professional career expert who backs them across a whole spectrum of career concerns (career coaching, job market analysis, CV writing, social media presence, tackling recruiters, interview coaching and salary negotiation) as well as helping them prepare for key promotions. Before I embarked on running my own business, I was a head-hunter and recruiter for 6 years and I filled mid-to-senior roles across financial services, FTSE 100, FTSE 250 and start-ups in the UK and abroad. My husband and I live in central London with 2 small girls (4 years old and almost 2). I hold dual nationality (Swedish/Scottish), have lived in 7 countries and visited an additional 45.

Since starting my business in January 2013 (and falling pregnant almost immediately afterwards) there have been 2 root causes to all my anxiety and stress (mental, physical, emotional and spiritual). They are the unpredictability of life (which effects productivity) and the lack of actual physical time. When I stopped fighting with these and instead made the conscious decision to embrace them, things changed a lot for the better.

These days I consciously strive to integrate and innovate the multiple demands that exist in my life as much as possible. A day that is won is a day that is productive. In practice, what does this actually mean? Let me share a page from my little black book of survival tricks.

- Get up at 5am to address urgent emails, tackle the laundry pile and plan the day ahead before the rest of the family wakes up.

- I keep one eye focused on the present and the second eye flicks ahead to the upcoming 48 hours. This way, as the hours unfold, I have already mentally worked out life's various logistics and administration and I respond better to unexpected events: heavy traffic, sick kids or client meetings at short notice.

- Mix up the car's entertainment on the school run so my girls and I listen to an eclectic mix of motivational talks, rock and pop music from 70s-2010s and Julia Donaldson's fantastic stories.

- I started something called "DoubleTime" where I meet up with various other mumpreneurs and talk about business and parental concerns while getting a manicure/pedicure at a local nail bar.

- My elder daughter and I often play a game that we call MSG where we share what happened in our days that made us Mad, Sad and Glad. It's a great way to bond, and it teaches my daughter the importance of acknowledging our feelings and that having good and bad days is normal.

- I end each day with a quick gratitude exercise which helps me to stay grounded, humble and positive.

This definitely doesn't happen every day but I do have fewer stressful days more frequently.

So, who am I truly?

A hat-stand that is hidden under a huge collection of virtual hats. I am a qualified career and life coach, ELI Master Practitioner (ELI is an innovative personality assessment), small business owner, mother, daughter, wife, friend, member of the Parent's Association, global citizen, animal lover, fan of ancient history, street art and flowers, and above all, a human being.

I am the one in whose handbag you will find my daughter's cuddly toy, some kid snacks and baby wipes in amongst my business card holder, laptop and work diary. I am the one in the café tapping my keyboard like mad to get work done in the precious time available before the school pick up. I am Victoria Fellowes, and I am just like you, another modern-day mumpreneur.

If you would like to meet a like-minded mumpreneur for coffee or want my professional help with your career, then either drop me an email at victoria@stride-forth.com or visit my website www.stride-forth.com

Kenny Akindele-Akande
(Dentist, A Life Performance Coach, Motivational Speaker,. Award Winning Author)

STAYING ON TOP OF YOUR GAME

A lot of times, failures are determined by past occurrence or life events. People beat themselves up over and over again over mistakes they cannot rewrite, which produces negative emotions that could burst the energy bubbles of the moment.

So life goes in a circle, from regrets of the past to the mistakes of the present and hereby leading to a failed future.

Hey, wake up from your sleep; it is a new day, a new dawn!

Not being able to separate the EVENTS of life FROM WHO YOU ARE is dangerous.

So you failed at something; it does not label you a FAILURE.

Hi, I'm Kenny Akande, and I just launched a bestseller book titled
"FINDING HAPPINESS. …Learn how to stay on top of your game in 30 days."

I am a wife, mother of two and a life coach. I can understand people, especially women or mothers, who are struggling to balance family, life and career.

Some women give up their career to nurture their children and family while some try to juggle the two together. No one is right or wrong, however the ability to have success in both is determined by DEFINING A BALANCE.

I found out that many women who stay at home struggle with unhappiness, identity crises, deflated energy etc.

Also some women with a career solely battle with the guilt of not being 100% available for their children and family. These women often miss important days and functions in their children's life. They blame themselves for their children's failure and laziness. They wish they were there for them.

Many other women fight depression, anxiety, or the loss of a husband, children and siblings, yet they are still expected to live and perform their best.

Therefore women are caught in the dilemma to either live or die. Those who succeed against all odds are not anything special, but they must have done things differently.

For 5 years now, I have helped women find inner peace, forgiveness and the strength to be the woman they desire to be. I would like to share the formula and secret I have applied in my coaching journey.

FORGIVENESS
FIGHT
FOCUS

Newton's third law of motion is, and I quote:

"For every action, there is an equal and opposite reaction".
Being swallowed up by failures, regrets, mistakes, denial, grief and guilt could lead to a retraction and deflation of energy. In order to overcome and to stay on top of these situations, one must launch an equal but opposite reaction according to Newton's law of motion. Therefore,

Where you are expected to feel weak, stay strong.
When moved to tears, wipe away your tears and ACT.
Where life wants you to stay down, LOOK UP.

SEVENTH LAW OF KARMA: LAW OF FOCUS

"It states that your mind cannot be in two places at once. When faced with anxiety, tragedy or loss, our immediate reaction is usually sadness or anger. As we grieve, our mind naturally seeks the positive. It is our choice if we want to continue to grieve for the rest of our days, or if we want to move past the pain, and be grateful for the experience. Even if the experience was painful, we can still be grateful for the lesson, and for the fact that it is over." ~Doe Zantamata

From this basic law, we understand that what you focus on expands, and what expands takes over space and control of our emotions. If this continues, it is going to swallow the victim up.

Therefore, it is imperative to make a CHOICE to STAY ON TOP and not give in.

I understand this does not come easy, but with INNER STRENGTH, FOCUS AND OVERWHELMING DESIRE FOR SUCCESS, you can achieve anything.

We cannot stop things from happening but we can choose how we want to react. Therefore,
FORGIVE YOUR PAST
FIND PEACE
FIND YOUR WORTH
DISCOVER TRUE HAPPINESS
Find your worth, inner peace and true happiness. Let nothing steal the beautiful future you desire for yourself. Don't hesitate to live out your dreams, don't wait for permission to breathe. LET NOTHING SWALLOW YOU UP BUT CHOOSE TO STAY ON TOP OF YOUR GAME.

Afia Miah
(BSc (Hons))

I'm the eldest of 4 siblings. Growing up, I didn't realise how hard our parents worked to raise us. It's easy to take parents for granted. It wasn't until I was blessed with children of my own that I realised how much my parents did and are still doing for us.

Before I had my first child, I was working full-time. I was able to return back to work full-time after 1 year of maternity leave. It was a very difficult time, but it was made easier because my husband changed his hours so he could look after our son while I was at work. The first weeks were hard, as my son used to cry when I was leaving. When I got home he would turn his head away and pretend to ignore me. Soon we all got into our routine.

After we had our second child, we decided the best thing for us was to move closer to my parents. Again, I returned to work full-time after 1 year off. My mum and husband were amazing; they did the school runs for my son and looked after my daughter.

A year later, I wanted to reduce my hours so I could do the school runs. I'm very grateful to everyone in my company for making it possible for me to do that. By working fewer hours I had lots more energy and time, so that was great!

The biggest struggle for me is keeping up with household

duties and getting things done on time.

Inspirational tips for other mumpreneurs

Aim high – Don't be afraid to have big dreams; we can all achieve so much if we try. With the right guidance, children can reach their full potential and inspire us to do more.

Be organised – Use whatever works for you. Use a family diary, calendar, planner, or your phone. Once your children start school there will be so many activities that you need to keep track of, and you'll feel bad if you forget something!

Do what's best – Don't compare yourself with others; make the right choices for you. Don't be afraid to make changes, just make sure you think everything through carefully.

Get involved – Take an active role in your child(ren)'s school by becoming a class representative, parent governor, or volunteering during events.

Learn to prioritise – Don't be hard on yourself. Decide what has to be done and do those things; everything else will just have to wait.

Make a routine – Decide how strict or flexible you want to be.

Take a break – Do something you enjoy. If you're happy, you'll be able to make others happy too.

Victoria Parker
(BSc and Executive Assistant)

I'm Victoria, 41 and not counting! I'm married to Stuart, and we have two children: Lois (6) and Casey (2). I went back to work full-time when Lois was seven months old, and she went to nursery. We deliberately waited a while to have another baby, as we couldn't afford childcare for two. While I was pregnant with Casey, my husband was made redundant. So, we decided that he would stay at home after the baby was born, and I would take a short maternity leave and return to work. I went back after three months. So, I've been a working mum for over 6 years.

I never saw myself as a full-time stay-at-home parent. I've worked at the same place since I left university. I've made a valuable role for myself, and I'd be reluctant to give it up. I'm fortunate to have a wonderful boss who is kind, thoughtful and flexible. I think it's important to remember that your employer deserves somebody who is committed and works hard. Make sound childcare arrangements, so that you can concentrate at work. That way you will be successful at work, and on the occasions when children have to come first, you won't feel guilty, and your boss will know that you have your priorities in order. My other coping mechanisms, both at home and at work, are just trying to generate positive energy, and to look for solutions rather than simply identify problems. Life is full of challenges and surprises, so I try to look for the best ways to handle things rather than wallow! When I went back to work after having my son, I knew that feeding might be a challenge. I expressed milk almost immediately. I always had a fridge and freezer full of milk, and my son was 100% breastmilk-fed until six months. I was so happy to do that, because I did feel slightly guilty about going back to work so soon. Providing the milk was important to me.

Worrying is natural when our children are out of our sight and/or control, and it can affect concentration and performance. It helps to have a trusted childcare plan in place. With my daughter I chose a nursery that was recommended, and which I visited while I was pregnant so that I could get a feel for the environment. My son is at home with his dad, so he gets full-time attention. You should allow yourself time to get used to being away from your children, and remember that it's OK to worry a bit. You're only human!

I sometimes struggle to give time to my family. I can be a bit of a workaholic. I am working on it (no pun intended!).

Tips or tools:

Take it one day at a time. Planning is sensible and exciting, but accept that you can't plan for everything.

Try not to absorb other people's negative energy. Negativity can be destructive, and their bad experiences are not necessarily going to be yours.

Try to achieve a balance. Have time for yourself. Do things that don't involve your children, because it's good for you and it's good for them. Working and having adult social time is not a crime.

Make informed decisions, be confident, and do what works for your family. You don't need everybody else's approval.

~CHAPTER 9~

GRATITUDE

Each and every one of us women are so incredibly different. I want to emphasize to all my readers that everyone is different and YOU are doing a fantastic job! Don't compare yourself to others. You do what's best and right for YOU.

YOU ARE DOING A GREAT JOB! BE PROUD OF WHO YOU ARE AND WHAT YOU HAVE ACHIEVED!

A lot of us tend to be so absorbed in thinking about how others are running a perfectly wonderful life that we don't stop to look at our own and embrace it.

STOP A MOMENT.
TAKE A DEEP BREATH.
PURE SILENCE AND BLISS.
LOOK AROUND YOU.
LOOK AT YOUR CHILDREN.
REMINISE ON YOUR ACHIEVEMENTS.

NOW WRITE DOWN 5 THINGS YOU'RE GRATEFUL FOR........DOESN'T THAT FEEL GOOD?

You will now realize how much you have in your life to be grateful for. By looking at your children, remember the time you birthed them. Yes, you made those wonderful things!

Be generous and appreciate yourself. Count your blessings; you have so many, only if you spend some time to take it all in.

As a mother, to be happy and successful you need to start believing in yourself and believe that what you're doing is worthwhile. It is the same concept for entrepreneurs: it will be challenging at the beginning but believe in your vision and it will come true.

Nothing can be accomplished without perseverance. Stay focused and committed to everything you do. As a mumpreneur you cannot substitute hard work. No one will do it for you. Just like you need to potty train your children, no one else can do it for you. The same concept applies to gratitude. You need to love and appreciate yourself first before anyone else can.

Gratitude will help you feel happier, more energized and focused and will improve your productivity.

At the back of the book I have compiled 365 motivational/gratitude quotations which you can read, one for each day, to inspire you to believe in yourself. Take 5 minutes out of your busy schedule to read one a day and write down your thoughts. You will be surprised by how this will change your attitude towards life. By doing so you will become more thankful and be grateful for everything around you!

Always remember: however you go about balancing your life, you're doing a great job and everybody does things differently. There is no set way. You choose what best suits you to succeed in life.

~CHAPTER 10~

AFFIRMATIONS

Make Today Amazing

There are so many of us who have negative thoughts such as "I'm never going to get this job done" and "I'm not good at doing that". When we start to doubt ourselves and allow negative thoughts to enter our minds, it takes a toll on our confidence. Our mood and outlook of life totally turn negative too. By having these negative thoughts we convince ourselves that we're not capable and not good enough. As a result, this affects our family and work life as well as our physical and mental health.

However, if we start implementing the opposite by allowing the positive thoughts to take over, automatically life will feel more relaxed and achievable.

In this chapter we will be covering how we can use affirmations to create a positive change in our work-life balance.

Affirmations are positive thoughts that will help you challenge and overcome the aura of negativity. By repeating the positive affirmations to yourself daily, you will begin to believe in yourself and create a positive change in your life.
Affirmations can be used in any situation, such as:

- When you're feeling frustrated, angry or impatient. It will help control your feelings and change your emotions into a positive outlook.
- When you want to improve your productivity. Reading the affirmations aloud will help you focus and be in control of yourself.
- Improving your self-esteem. You will feel more confident, a sense of determination and positivity about life.

To get the best results out of affirmations you should combine positive thinking with goal setting.

There are several techniques you can use: Some people prefer to write out their affirmations on sticky notes and stick them around the house so that they can be visually motivating. Some people like to read them out aloud, and some prefer to write the affirmations over and over again. Some do all three. You do what works for YOU!

In terms of goal setting, it will allow you to think about your personal goals and drive you to achieve them. You should repeat the affirmations every day and also after any negative thoughts. Slowly, you will find yourself feeling more relaxed and in control of any situation.

If you're struggling with a specific area in life or behavior, you can use affirmations to turn the negatives into positives. When you're writing your affirmations, make sure you write them in the present tense. This will help you to feel as if they're happening right now. Read them aloud and say them with determination. You have to believe them, so make them realistic and achievable.

I've put together a few positive affirmations you could use.

I AM SUCCESSFUL

I AM A GREAT MUM

I BELIEVE IN MYSELF

I AM GRATEFUL

I AM HAPPY

I AM BLESSED WITH AN INCREDIBLE FAMILY

MY LIFE IS JUST BEGINNING

- Affirmations -

I am amazing and I love how I'm always so enthusiastic!

I am a star!

Aim high! Follow your dreams!

I am successful

I live in the present and am confident of the future.

I am doing my best and that is always enough

I have the power to create change

I feel powerful, capable, confident, energetic, and on top of the world.

I believe in myself and in my abilities

I can and I will

All is well right now.

I am grateful for this moment and find joy in it.

I breath in relaxation. I breath out stress.

I feel grateful for everything I have in my life

I am completely pain free, and my body is full of energy.

By allowing myself to be happy, I inspire others to be happy as well.

I look at the world around me and can't help but smile and feel joy.

I choose to be proud of myself.

I know exactly what I need to do to achieve success.

~ABOUT THE AUTHOR~

Labosshy Mayooran is a graduate of Master's in Research (MRes) in Translational Medicine from Imperial College London. Whilst undertaking her master's she published "The Effects of Kisspeptin-10 on Reproductive Hormone Release Show Sexual Dimorphism in Humans J Clin Endocrinol Metab 2011; 96 E1963-E1972". Labosshy has also attained a Bachelor's (BSc (Hons)) degree in Biomedical Sciences from Queen Mary University London.

She lives in England and is married to Mayooran Senthilmani, who is an award winning author, Finance Director as well as the Founder and CEO of DVG star Ltd and the Co-founder of Universal Learning Academy. Labosshy is currently a mum to 2 adorable boys, Jaison who is 2 and half years old and Mylesh who is 6 months old at the time of writing this book, and she is also an entrepreneur. Thus the term 'mumpreneur'. She is the Managing Director and Co-founder of Universal Learning Academy, which is an online learning platform. Labosshy worked at Hammersmith Medicines Research (Private phase I and II clinical trials company) for over 5 years, and had the role of Quality Research Associate and Trial Monitor.

Her hobbies are watching inspirational movies, dancing and spending time with her family. Labosshy is a renowned dancer and has completed a Diploma in Bharatanatiyam (South Indian

Classical dance) as well as Grade 7 in Veena (a South Indian classical instrument).

Labosshy is a young and versatile individual, who is driven by hard work and challenges. She has always been a committed team player with good leadership qualities and is known for her keen eye for detail. Being a mum, she always prioritizes her children over anything else and aims to be a good role model for them.

Her goal and dream is to inspire future and present mums to develop a positive attitude to life and to raise their self-beliefs for greater achievement. She strives to help them understand that life may bring struggles but we all have the will power to overcome the obstacles, and have the confidence in ourselves that we are doing our best. She wants to inspire mothers to be grateful to be mothers as children are such a blessing. And she wants all mums to remember that however you tackle the challenges you face, your way is best for you and your family. You're doing a great job!

365

D A Y S   O F   G R A T I T U D E

Here are 365 motivational/gratitude quotes, one for every day of the year, to inspire you to believe in yourself. Read the quotation, have a think and then write down your thoughts and how the quote fits into your life.

1. "Optimism is the faith that leads to achievement."
   - Helen Keller

2. "You are the one that possesses the keys to your being. You carry the passport to your own happiness."
   - Diane von Furstenberg

3. "Make the most of yourself by fanning the tiny, inner sparks of possibility into flames of achievement."- Golda Meir

4. "I didn't get there by wishing for it or hoping for it, but by working for it." - Estée Lauder

5. "You can never leave footprints that last if you are always walking on tiptoe." - Leymah Gbowee

6. "Step out of the history that is holding you back. Step into the new story you are willing to create." - Oprah Winfrey

7. "I choose to make the rest of my life the best of my life."
   - Louise Hay

8. "Change your life today. Don't gamble on the future, act now, without delay." - Simone de Beauvoir

9. "Doubt is a killer. You just have to know who you are and what you stand for."- Jennifer Lopez

10. "Hold your head and your standards high even as people or circumstances try to pull you down." - Tory Johnson

11. "I learned a long time ago that there is something worse than missing the goal, and that's not pulling the trigger."
    - Mia Hamm

12. "If you don't get out of the box you've been raised in, you won't understand how much bigger the world is."
    - Angelina Jolie

13. "We do not need magic to change the world, we carry all the power we need inside ourselves already: we have the power to imagine better." - J.K. Rowling

14. "When I'm tired, I rest. I say, 'I can't be a superwoman today.'" - Jada Pinkett Smith

15. "You get in life what you have courage to ask for."
    – Oprah Winfrey

16. "Being happy doesn't mean everything is perfect. It means you've decided to look beyond the imperfections."
    - Anonymous

17. "Successful mothers are not the ones who have never struggled. They are the ones who never give up, despite the struggles."
    – Sharon Jaynes

18. "There is no way to be perfect one but a million ways to be a good one."
    – Anonymous

19. "Being a mother is not about what you gave up to have a child, but what you've gained from having one."
    – Sunny Gupta

20. "There will be so many times you feel like you've failed but in the eyes, heart and mind of your child you are super mom." – Stephanie Precourt

21. "Focus on being productive instead of busy." - Tim Ferris

22. "The 3 C's in life: Choice, Chance, Change. You must make the choice, to take the chance if you want anything in life to change." - Anonymous

23. "Life is not measured by the number of breaths we take, but by the moments that take our breath away." – Maya Angelou

24. "A woman is like a tea bag – you never know how strong she is until she gets in hot water." – Eleanor Roosevelt

25. "A woman is the full circle. Within her is the power to create, nurture and transform." – Diane Mariechild

26. "Success breeds confidence." – Beryl Markham

27. "The way in which we think of ourselves has everything to do with how our world see us and how we see ourselves successfully acknowledged by the world." – Arlene Rankin

28. "If you look at what you have in life, you'll always have more. If you look at what you don't have in life, you'll never have enough." – Oprah Winfrey

29. "You can have unbelievable intelligence, you can have connections, you can have opportunities fall out of the sky. But in the end, hard work is the true, enduring characteristic of successful people." – Marsha Evans

30. "You have to have confidence in your ability, and then be tough enough to follow through." – Rosalynn Carter

31. "Let us be grateful to the people who make us happy; they are the charming gardeners who make our souls blossom." - Marcel Proust

32. "Gratitude makes sense of our past, brings peace for today, and creates a vision for tomorrow. " - Melody Beattie

33. "As we express our gratitude, we must never forget that the highest appreciation is not to utter words, but to live by them" - John F. Kennedy

34. "Happiness cannot be traveled to, owned, earned, worn or consumed. Happiness is the spiritual experience of living every minute with love, grace, and gratitude" - Denis Waitley

35. "Develop an attitude of gratitude, and give thanks for everything that happens to you, knowing that every step forward is a step toward achieving something bigger and better than your current situation" - Brian Tracy

36. "I think I run my strongest when I run with joy, with gratitude, with focus, with grace. " – Kristin Armstrong

37. "Gratitude can transform common days into thanksgivings, turn routine jobs into joy, and change ordinary opportunities into blessings" - William Arthur Ward

38. "Gratitude unlocks the fullness of life. It turns what we have into enough, and more. It turns denial into acceptance, chaos to order, confusion to clarity. It can turn a meal into a feast, a house into a home, a stranger into a friend." - Melody Beattie

39. "I don't have to chase extraordinary moments to find happiness - it's right in front of me if I'm paying attention and practicing gratitude" - Brene Brown

40. "'Thank you' is the best prayer that anyone could say. I say that one a lot. Thank you expresses extreme gratitude, humility, understanding" - Alice Walker

41. "True forgiveness is when you can say, "Thank you for that experience." - Oprah Winfrey

42. "Start each day with a positive thought and a grateful heart."
- Roy T. Bennett,

43. "At the end of the day, let there be no excuses, no explanations, no regrets." - Steve Maraboli,

44. "Gratitude is the fairest blossom which springs from the soul." - Henry Ward Beecher

45. "Nature's beauty is a gift that cultivates appreciation and gratitude" - Louie Schwartzberg

46. "No one who achieves success does so without acknowledging the help of others. The wise and confident acknowledge this help with gratitude"
- Alfred North Whitehead

47. "When a person doesn't have gratitude, something is missing in his or her humanity. A person can almost be defined by his or her attitude toward gratitude "- Elie Wiesel

48. "Joy is the simplest form of gratitude" - Karl Barth

49. "As you keep your mind and heart focused in the right direction, approaching each day with faith and gratitude, I believe you will be empowered to live life to the fullest and enjoy the abundant life He has promised you!"
- Victoria Osteen

50. "When we focus on our gratitude, the tide of disappointment goes out and the tide of love rushes in." - Kristin Armstrong

51. "Thankfulness is the beginning of gratitude. Gratitude is the completion of thankfulness. Thankfulness may consist merely of words. Gratitude is shown in acts".
- Henri Frederic Amiel

52. "A smart manager will establish a culture of gratitude. Expand the appreciative attitude to suppliers, vendors, delivery people, and of course, customers." -Harvey Mackay

53. "Gratitude helps you to grow and expand; gratitude brings joy and laughter into your life and into the lives of all those around you" - Eileen Caddy

54. "Feeling gratitude and not expressing it is like wrapping a present and not giving it." - William Arthur Ward

55. "Enjoy the little things, for one day you may look back and realize they were the big things." - Robert Brault

56. "As we express our gratitude, we must never forget that the highest appreciation is not to utter words but to live by them." - John F. Kennedy

57. "Reflect upon your present blessings, of which every man has plenty; not on your past misfortunes, of which all men have some." - Charles Dickens

58. "Acknowledging the good that you already have in your life is the foundation for all abundance." - Eckhart Tolle

59. "If a fellow isn't thankful for what he's got, he isn't likely to be thankful for what he's going to get." - Frank A. Clark

60. "If you want to turn your life around, try thankfulness. It will change your life mightily." - Gerald Good

61. "Gratitude turns what we have into enough, and more. It turns denial into acceptance, chaos into order, confusion into clarity...it makes sense of our past, brings peace for today, and creates a vision for tomorrow." - Melody Beattie

62. "Gratitude is a currency that we can mint for ourselves, and spend without fear of bankruptcy."
- Fred De Witt Van Amburgh

63. "The way to develop the best that is in a person is by appreciation and encouragement." - Charles Schwab

64. "He is a wise man who does not grieve for the things which

he has not, but rejoices for those which he has." -Epictetus

65. "At times, our own light goes out and is rekindled by a spark from another person. Each of us has cause to think with deep gratitude of those who have lighted the flame within us." - Albert Schweitzer

66. "The deepest craving of human nature is the need to be appreciated." - William James

67. "Be thankful for what you have; you'll end up having more. If you concentrate on what you don't have, you will never, ever have enough." - Oprah Winfrey

68. "Let us rise up and be thankful, for if we didn't learn a lot today, at least we learned a little, and if we didn't learn a little, at least we didn't get sick, and if we got sick, at least we didn't die; so, let us all be thankful." – Buddha

69. "Silent gratitude isn't very much to anyone." - Gertrude Stein

70. "Thankfulness is the beginning of gratitude. Gratitude is the completion of thankfulness. Thankfulness may consist merely of words. Gratitude is shown in acts."
- Henri Frederic Amiel

71. "You cannot do a kindness too soon because you never know how soon it will be too late." - Ralph Waldo Emerson

72. "When I started counting my blessings, my whole life turned around." - Willie Nelson

73. "It is impossible to feel grateful and depressed in the same moment." - Naomi Williams

74. "One can never pay in gratitude; one can only pay 'in kind' somewhere else in life." - Anne Morrow Lindbergh

75. "Things turn out best for people who make the best of the way things turn out." - John Wooden

76. "No one who achieves success does so without the help of others. The wise and confident acknowledge this help with gratitude." - Alfred North Whitehead

77. "Piglet noticed that even though he had a Very Small Heart, it could hold a rather large amount of Gratitude." - A.A. Milne

78. "Forget yesterday--it has already forgotten you. Don't sweat tomorrow--you haven't even met. Instead, open your eyes and your heart to a truly precious gift--today."
    - Steve Maraboli

79. "We should certainly count our blessings, but we should also make our blessings count." - Neal A. Maxwell

80. "In ordinary life, we hardly realize that we receive a great deal more than we give, and that it is only with gratitude that life becomes rich." - Dietrich Bonhoeffer

81. "The only people with whom you should try to get even are those who have helped you." - John E. Southard

82. "Gratitude also opens your eyes to the limitless potential of the universe, while dissatisfaction closes your eyes to it."
    - Stephen Richards

83. "Gratitude and attitude are not challenges; they are choices."
    - Robert Braathe

84. "Gratitude is more of a compliment to yourself than someone else." - Raheel Farooq

85. "Keep your eyes open and try to catch people in your company doing something right, then praise them for it."
    - Tom Hopkins

86. "In life, one has a choice to take one of two paths: to wait for some special day--or to celebrate each special day."
    - Rasheed Ogunlaru

87. "This a wonderful day. I've never seen this one before."
    - Maya Angelou

88. "Gratitude is the healthiest of all human emotions. The more
    you express gratitude for what you have, the more likely you
    will have even more to express gratitude for." - Zig Ziglar

89. "Learn to be thankful for what you already have, while you
    pursue all that you want." - Jim Rohn

90. "Be thankful for what you have; you'll end up having more. If
    you concentrate on what you don't have, you will never, ever
    have enough." - Oprah Winfrey

91. "Thank you' is the best prayer that anyone could say. I say
    that one a lot. Thank you expresses extreme gratitude,
    humility, understanding." - Alice Walker

92. "The way to develop the best that is in a person is by
    appreciation and encouragement." - Charles Schwab

93. "When I started counting my blessings, my whole life turned
    around." - Willie Nelson

94. "The roots of all goodness lie in the soil of appreciation for
    goodness." - Dalai Lama

95. "Reflect upon your present blessings, of which every man has
    plenty; not on your past misfortunes, of which all men have
    some." - Charles Dickens

96. "Gratitude always comes into play; research shows that
    people are happier if they are grateful for the positive things
    in their lives, rather than worrying about what might be
    missing." - Dan Buettner

97. "There are only two ways to live your life. One is as though
    nothing is a miracle. The other is as though everything is a
    miracle." - Albert Einstein

98. "No duty is more urgent than that of returning thanks."
    – James Allen

99. "Some people grumble that roses have thorns; I am grateful
    that thorns have roses." – Alphonse Karr

100. Saying thank you is more than good manners. It is good
     spirituality. – Alfred Painter

101. "Appreciation is a wonderful thing. It makes what is
     excellent in others belong to us as well." – Voltaire

102. "Cultivate the habit of being grateful for every good thing
     that comes to you, and to give thanks continuously." – Ralph
     Waldo Emerson

103. "Let us be grateful to people who make us happy."
     – Marcel Proust

104. "Giving is an expression of gratitude for our blessings."
     – Laura Arrillaga-Andreessen

105. "We must learn to accept who we are and appreciate who
     we become. We must love ourselves for what and who we
     are, and believe in our talents." - Harley King

106. "We forget to see the blessings of the day. Because of this,
     our spirit is poisoned instead of nourished." - Steve Maraboli

107. "Happiness is not a thing – it is a feeling; a way of joyful
     living and being. It comes from inner fulfillment and
     appreciating the world you live in."- Rasheed Ogunlaru

108. "Appreciate what you have been given and you will be
     promoted higher." - Israelmore Ayivor

109. "Everything in life is given to you for a short period of time,
     to enjoy, to learn from, to appreciate and to love, but never
     to keep." - Luminita D. Saviuc

110. "Hopeful thinking can get you out of your fear zone and into your appreciation zone." - Martha Beck

111. "People, places, and experiences aren't meant to be labeled and judged, they are meant to be loved and appreciated, since deep down inside, the nature we all share is love, light, and happiness." - Luminita D. Saviuc

112. "Nature's beauty is a gift that cultivates appreciation and gratitude." - Louie Schwartzberg

113. "Be thankful for everything that happens in your life; it's all an experience." - Roy T. Bennett

114. "True love is not in possessions or obsessions; it is in appreciation." - Debasish Mridha

115. "You never fully appreciate what you had until you don't have it anymore" - Glenn Beck

116. "When we set expectations and nourish them with appreciation, we will get better results."- Debasish Mridha

117. "We must find time to stop and thank the people who make a difference in our lives."- John F. Kennedy

118. "When one has a grateful heart, life is so beautiful."
     - Roy T. Bennett

119. "You pray in your distress and in your need; would that you might pray also in the fullness of your joy and in your days of abundance." - Kahlil Gibran

120. "It doesn't matter what you did or where you were...it matters where you are and what you're doing. Get out there! Sing the song in your heart and NEVER let anyone shut you up!!" - Steve Maraboli

121. "Gratitude is not only the greatest of virtues, but the parent of all others." - Marcus Tullius Cicero

122. "When you arise in the morning, think of what a precious privilege it is to be alive—to breathe, to think, to enjoy, to love—then make that day count!" - Steve Maraboli

123. "Appreciation is a wonderful thing. It makes what is excellent in others belong to us as well." - Voltaire

124. "As we express our gratitude, we must never forget that the highest appreciation is not to utter words, but to live by them" - John F. Kennedy

125. "Those with a grateful mindset tend to see the message in the mess. And even though life may knock them down, the grateful find reasons, if even small ones, to get up."
- Steve Maraboli

126. "Free yourself from the complexities and drama of your life. Simplify. Look within. Within ourselves we all have the gifts and talents we need to fulfill the purpose we've been blessed with." - Steve Maraboli

127. "In normal life we hardly realize how much more we receive than we give, and life cannot be rich without such gratitude. It is so easy to overestimate the importance of our own achievements compared with what we owe to the help of others." - Dietrich Bonhoeffer

128. "We should certainly count our blessings, but we should also make our blessings count." - Neal A. Maxwell

129. "The unthankful heart discovers no mercies; but the thankful heart will find, in every hour, some heavenly blessings." - Henry Ward Beecher

130. "Gratitude can transform common days into thanksgivings, turn routine jobs into joy, and change ordinary opportunities into blessings." - William Arthur Ward

131. "We don't truly appreciate what we have until it's gone. We don't really appreciate something until we have experienced

some events; we don't really appreciate our parents until we ourselves have become parents. Be grateful for what you have now, and nothing should be taken for granted."
- Roy T. Bennett

132. "Gratitude looks to the Past and love to the Present; fear, avarice, lust, and ambition look ahead."- C.S. Lewis,

133. "When you are grateful, fear disappears and abundance appears." - Anthony Robbins

134. "Be happy with who you are and what you do, and you can do anything you want." - Steve Maraboli

135. "Feeling gratitude and not expressing it is like wrapping a present and not giving it." - William Arthur Ward

136. "Although time seems to fly, it never travels faster than one day at a time. Each day is a new opportunity to live your life to the fullest. In each waking day, you will find scores of blessings and opportunities for positive change. Do not let your TODAY be stolen by the unchangeable past or the indefinite future! Today is a new day!"- Steve Maraboli

137. "Those who have the ability to be grateful are the ones who have the ability to achieve greatness." - Steve Maraboli

138. "What separates privilege from entitlement is gratitude."
- Brené Brown

139. "In ordinary life we hardly realize that we receive a great deal more than we give, and that it is only with gratitude that life becomes rich." - Dietrich Bonhoeffer

140. "The greatest wisdom is in simplicity. Love, respect, tolerance, sharing, gratitude, forgiveness. It's not complex or elaborate. The real knowledge is free. It's encoded in your DNA. All you need is within you. Great teachers have said that from the beginning. Find your heart, and you will find your way." - Carlos Barrios

141. "An attitude of gratitude brings great things." - Yogi Bhajan

142. "A grateful mindset can set you free from the prison of disempowerment and the shackles of misery."
- Steve Maraboli

143. "If you want to find happiness, find gratitude."
- Steve Maraboli

144. "We only live once. We all have an expiration date after that we will never come again. I am not saying that to make you sad. I am saying that so you can cherish each moment in your life and be grateful that you are here and you are Special"
- Pablo

145. "Take full account of what Excellencies you possess, and in gratitude remember how you would hanker after them, if you had them not." - Marcus Aurelius

146. "Gratitude is the ability to experience life as a gift. It liberates us from the prison of self-preoccupation."
- John Ortberg

147. "When you express gratitude for the blessings that come into your life, it not only encourages the universe to send you more, it also sees to it that those blessings remain."
- Stephen Richards

148. "When it comes to life the critical thing is whether you take things for granted or take them with gratitude."
- G.K. Chesterton

149. "Be happy, noble heart, be blessed for all the good thou hast done and wilt do hereafter, and let my gratitude remain in obscurity like your good deeds." - Alexandre Dumas

150. "Thankfulness creates gratitude which generates contentment that causes peace." - Todd Stocker

151. "Your dream is a reality that is waiting for you to

materialize. Today is a new day! Don't let your history
interfere with your destiny! Learn from your past so that it
can empower your present and propel you to greatness"
- Steve Maraboli

152. "Gratitude for the seemingly insignificant—a seed—this
plants the giant miracle." - Ann Voskamp

153. "A little "thank you" that you will say to someone for a
"little favour" shown to you is a key to unlock the doors that
hide unseen "greater favours". Learn to say "thank you" and
why not?" - Israelmore Ayivor

154. "Gratitude paints little smiley faces on everything it
touches." - Richelle E. Goodrich

155. "If we want to keep the blessings of life coming to us, we
must learn to be grateful for whatever is given."
- Harold Klemp

156. "Be consistent in your dedication to showing your gratitude
to others. Gratitude is a fuel, a medicine, and spiritual and
emotional nourishment."- Steve Maraboli

157. "Always remember people who have helped you along the
way, and don't forget to lift someone up." - Roy Bennett

158. "Gratitude always comes into play; research shows that
people are happier if they are grateful for the positive things
in their lives, rather than worrying about what might be
missing." -Dan Buettner

159. "Gratitude and love are always multiplied when you give
freely. It is an infinite source of contentment and prosperous
energy." - Jim Fargiano

160. "Gratitude is an overflow of the pleasure filling your soul."
- Raheel Farooq

161. "Most of us forget to take time for wonder, praise and

gratitude until it is almost too late. Gratitude is a many-colored quality, reaching in all directions. It goes out for small things and for large; it is a God-ward going."
- Faith Baldwin

162. "Summoning gratitude is a sure way to get our life back on track. Opening our eyes to affirm gratitude grows the garden of our inner abundance, just as standing close to a fire eventually warms our heart." - Alexandra Katehakis

163. "The soul that gives thanks can find comfort in everything; the soul that complains can find comfort in nothing."
- Hannah Whitall Smith

164. "When you focus on gratitude, positive things flow in more readily, making you even more grateful."
- Lissa Rankin

165. "Life is a web of intersections and choices. Your 1st choice is to recognize an intersection. Your 2nd choice is to be grateful for it." - Ryan Lilly

166. "Start each day with a positive thought and a grateful heart."
- Roy Bennett

167. "Be grateful for what you already have while you pursue what you want." - Roy Bennett

168. "Gratitude builds a bridge to abundance." - Roy Bennett

169. "Be grateful for what you already have while you pursue your goals." - Roy Bennett

170. "Don't count your blessings, let your blessings count! Enjoy Life!" - Bernard Kelvin Clive

171. "Gratitude also opens your eyes to the limitless potential of the universe, while dissatisfaction closes your eyes to it."
- Stephen Richards

172. "For a wise man, I have been told, once said, 'Gratitude is best and most effective when it does not evaporate in empty phrases.' But alas, my lady, I am but a mass of empty phrases, it would seem." - Isaac Asimov

173. "Life-changing gratitude does not fasten to a life unless nailed through with one very specific nail at a time."
- Ann Voskamp

174. "When the gratitude of many to one throws away all shame, we behold fame." - Friedrich Nietzsche

175. "No one can obtain felicity by pursuit. This explains why one of the elements of being happy is the feeling that a debt of gratitude is owed, a debt impossible to pay. Now, we do not owe gratitude to ourselves. To be conscious of gratitude is to acknowledge a gift." - Josef Pieper

176. "Expectation has brought me disappointment. Disappointment has brought me wisdom. Acceptance, gratitude and appreciation have brought me joy and fulfilment." - Rasheed Ogunlaru

177. "Rather than getting more spoilt with age, as difficulties pile up, epiphanies of gratitude abound." - Alain de Botton

178. "Living the dream." - Tom Giaquinto

179. "Be thankful for the efforts of people who worked hard to get you where you are; you should not take it for granted and treat them with indifference." - Roy T. Bennett

180. "Each day brings new opportunities, allowing you to constantly live with love—be there for others—bring a little light into someone's day. Be grateful and live each day to the fullest." - Roy Bennett

181. "Making the ungrateful grateful is a tedious endeavor."
- Ana Monnar

182. "Grateful people are happy people. The more things you are grateful for, the happier you will be." - Roy T. Bennett

183. "Though they only take a second to say, thank yous leave a warm feeling behind that can last for hours."
- Kent Allan Rees

184. "The more grateful we are, the more we practice this in our everyday lives, the more connected we become to the universe around us." - Stephen Richards

185. "I try hard to hold fast to the truth that a full and thankful heart cannot entertain great conceits. When brimming with gratitude, one's heartbeat must surely result in outgoing love, the finest emotion we can ever know." - Bill W.

186. "More Miracles occur from Gratitude and Forgiveness than anything else" - Philip H. Friedman

187. "Embrace every new day with gratitude, hope and love."
- Lailah Gifty Akita

188. "Be grateful for whatever it is that opens you up."
- Allan G. Hunter

189. "Gratitude is a form of worship in its own right, as it implies the acceptance of a power greater than yourself."
- Stephen Richards

190. "One may suffer the long-term in order to grow in appreciation for the small things. For in short-term suffering, one only notices the large."- Criss Jami

191. "That very breath wherewith they utter their complaints is a blessing and a fundamental one too for if God would withdraw that they were incapable of whatsoever else either have or desire." - Richard Allestree

192. "Think not so much of what you lack as of what you have: but of the things that you have, select the best, and then

reflect on how eagerly you would have sought them if you did not have them." - Marcus Aurelius

193. "Gratitude is one of the most powerful human emotions. Once expressed, it changes attitude, brightens outlook, and broadens our perspective." - Germany Kent

194. "Take time daily to reflect on how much you have. It may not be all that you want but remember someone somewhere is dreaming to have what you have." - Germany Kent

195. "To become a better you, remember to be grateful to people who have contributed to making you who you are today." - Israelmore Ayivor

196. "Loyalty starts with a demonstration of respect and gratitude." - Chip Bell

197. "When you feel thankful, you can be appreciative for a moment, then not at all the next. It seems the tank is full, then it becomes empty, and the cycle continues. If you don't feel the same gratitude for a moment, know that it's possible in the next moment that comes around." - J.R. Rim

198. "Any day above ground is a good day. Before you complain about anything, be thankful for your life and the things that are still going well." - Germany Kent

199. "Don't ever stop believing in your own transformation. It is still happening even on days you may not realize it or feel like it." - Lalah Delia

200. "Gratitude houses plenitude amidst scarcity." - Sravani Saha Nakhro

201. "Take time daily to reflect on how much you have. It may not be all that you want but remember someone somewhere is dreaming of what you own." - Germany Kent

202. "Gratitude will make you feel great, choose to be grateful."
- Gift Gugu Mona

203. "Inhale grace, exhale gratitude." - Sravani Saha Nakhro

204. "I choose to say it is well even when it is not, because in every situation I find myself in, I still learn from it."
- Gift Gugu Mona

205. "In an expression of attitude or building character, we forgot real gratitude. In an artificial expression, we lost our real identity and longing to become something, it's never ending process. So, are you willing to look inside? And take the journey from attitude to gratitude." - Abhinav Rajput

206. "An attitude of gratitude increases abundance and diminishes fear." - Jeffrey Fry

207. "Happy people tend to be those who take pleasure in simple things." - Auliq Ice

208. "Being grateful for what you have is the key to peace and happiness." - Pravin Agarwal

209. "Gratitude is a miracle of its own recognition. It brings out a sense of appreciation and sincerity of a being." - Auliq-Ice

210. "Gratitude turns disappointment into lessons learned, discoveries made, alternatives explored, and new plans set in motion." - Auliq-Ice

211. "For the grateful, there is no room for disappointment; Each moment offers life." - Auliq-Ice

212. "Count your blessings as the more you are grateful for what you have the more there is to be grateful for."
- Pravin Agarwal

213. "Gratitude gets us through the hard stuff...Gratitude always leaves us looking at God and away from dread."
- Max Lucado

214. "Gratitude is the appreciation of things that are not deserved, earned or demanded - those wonderful things that we take for granted." - Renée Paule

215. "Express gratitude for every little thing."- Debasish Mridha

216. "Gratitude is a powerful trait."- Auliq-Ice

217. "She did not even trouble herself much to show Godfrey her gratitude. We may spoil gratitude as we offer it, by insisting on its recognition. To receive honestly is the best thanks for a good thing."- George MacDonald

218. "One should be glad for every breath one can take in this world." - Marty Rubin

219. "It's up to us to choose contentment and thankfulness now—and to stop imagining that we have to have everything perfect before we'll be happy." - Joanna Gaines

220. "Gratitude is a powerful catalyst for happiness. It's the spark that lights a fire of joy in your soul." - Amy Collette

221. "Gratitude unlocks the door of opportunities, blessing, greatness and prosperity. Gratitude is your key to a worthy life." - Sesan Kareem

222. "Be grateful for the day and the day will be grateful for you. Stay positive and everything around you will respond in kind." - TemitOpe Ibrahim

223. "The attitude of gratitude gives you the right rectitude and sound attitude towards life" - Sesan Kareem

224. "Your attitude of gratitude will bring you altitude in business and multitude in blessings." - Farshad Asl

225. "Only having valued a thing, can you truly be thankful. You cannot be sincerely thankful for what you have not valued."
- TemitOpe Ibrahim

226. "Gratitude is one of the virtues of the noble man. It is the hallmark of a life lived well. It is a trademark of the righteous man. It is an attribute that significantly impacts on your personal happiness and how sound your relationship will be with others." - Sesan Kareem

227. "Love and gratitude offers courage." - Auliq-Ice

228. "A generous heart filled with gratitude is a magnet for abundance." - Debasish Mridha

229. "The number one joy indicator, the one thing that will predict whether someone feels joy in their life or not, is the practice of gratitude." - John O'Leary

230. "Joy is the net of love by which we can capture souls. God loves the person who gives with joy. Whoever gives with joy gives more. The best way to show our gratitude to God and to people is to accept with joy." - Mother Teresa

231. "Don't over-focus on the negatives and under-focus the positives in your life." - Lalah Delia

232. "We cannot fully heal if we cannot experience gratitude on a daily basis." - Sharon E. Rainey

233. "Don't let your 'future success' dim the beauty and light that's in front of you right now." - Taryn Garland

234. "Life works with balance. If you give and receive out of giving, you create a balance with life. You serve life, before you expect life to serve you."- Roshan Sharma

235. "Success depends on your attitude; happiness depends on your gratitude." - Debasish Mridha

236. "The best way to achieve great success is to learn from wise people. Use them extensively with love, gratitude, and humility." - Debasish Mridha

237. "Always recompense kindness with hearty love and gratitude." - Debasish Mridha

238. "Once we forget those who have contributed time and effort in making an endeavor successful, we forget ourselves." - Beem Weeks

239. "Gratitude does not mean the absence of solitude, but the presence of a positive attitude in spite of."
- Gift Gugu Mona

240. "The things that people were the most grateful for were the ordinary things in life. The sound of your spouse's laugh, the smell of morning coffee, the echo of children playing in the yard. The little things. In waiting for the big moments—the vacations, the retirements, the birthdays—we risk missing the experiences of life most worthy of celebrating."
- John O'Leary

241. "Successes are those highlights of life we look back on with a smile. But it's the day to day grind of getting them that defines the laugh lines etched until the end of time. Enjoy each moment along the way" - Aaron Lauritsen

242. "Life-giving ministry flows from lives that are full of gratitude to God, not with an expectation of gratitude from others. In community we can support one another, affirm contributions and yet also trust that our work is sustained by grace." - Christopher L. Heuertz

243. "Gratitude is a way of life. Gratitude is the way home."
- Angie karan

244. "Love, positivity and gratitude are the most essential ingredients to a happy and fulfilled life." - Eileen Anglin

245. "Aim for happiness because if you keep looking to reach perfection, you're never going to appreciate anything."
- Karen A. Baquiran

246. "Cicero said that gratitude is not only the greatest of virtues, but the parent of all others. If that's true, then my happiness does not cause me to be grateful for what I have. My gratitude for what I have causes me to be happy. Gratitude births the virtue of happiness." - Jennifer Dukes Lee

247. "You must understand that it is not in the nature of Man to be grateful. So in whatever you or I do for others we must never expect gratitude. If we do, we will only be disappointed." - S R Nathan

248. "Keep your Eyes on All that's Good and Beautiful and Possible in the World. Because "The Stories We Tell Create the People We Become." - Jacqueline Lewis

249. "While the classic conversion story involves desperation, hitting bottom, and a plea for help, I think now that it was gratitude, as well as the suffering I'd seen, that made room for me to open my heart to something new." - Sara Miles

250. "We can never bring anything to us unless we are grateful for what we have. In fact, if somebody were completely and utterly grateful for everything, they would never have to ask for anything, because it would be given to them before they even asked."- Rhonda Byrne

251. "When a leader has an attitude of gratitude, it can create great differences in the lives of others."- Debasish Mridha

252. "In the modern world we are surrounded by so much abundance that we cannot see it." - Chris Matakas

253. "Everything you have ever done has led up to this very moment. Savor your life, the lessons, the wisdom, the failures, the victories and all the relationships that have made an imprint in your journey." - Karen A. Baquiran

254. "Start your day by awakening early to welcome the morning sun with a smile, love, and gratitude."- Debasish Mridha

255. "If I only looked at what I've lost, I'd never be able to see what I have." - Cindy Charlton

256. "The whole purpose of education is to create a window of the mind through which you can see the world. Look through that window with your own profound love, joy, harmony, and gratitude." - Debasish Mridha

257. "You can't be passionate about gratitude and be crippled by ingratitude."- Bamigboye Olurotimi

258. "The essential attributes of a great leader are a positive attitude, humility, and gratitude."- Debasish Mridha

259. "Always be grateful for life, love, and joy."
- Debasish Mridha

260. "Start each morning with appreciation, love, and gratitude."
- Debasish Mridha

261. "Silence your mind and breathe. Take this moment to show gratitude for the abundance of blessings in your life."
- Karen A. Baquiran

262. "Humanity reveals her inner beauty through the interplay of gratitude, love, and kindness."- Debasish Mridha

263. "Gratitude was never a noun; it's secretly a verb. It is not a place you accept defeat, settle in for broken dreams or call it the best life will get. Gratitude is getting out of laziness, self-pity, denial and insecurity, in order to walk through that door God has been holding open for you this entire time."
- Shannon L. Alder

264. "Embrace compassion without exception."
- Janice Anderson

265. "Don't waste all today worrying about the possible mistakes you may have made yesterday. You don't know what will happen tomorrow or how long we have here, so enjoy what you have today since you have it. May you be thankful for today and live it to the fullest as it truly is a gift"
- Angie karan

266. "Behind every creative act is a statement of love. Every artistic creation is a statement of gratitude."
- Kilroy J. Oldster

267. "As you lay yourself down to sleep tonight, think of something you are grateful for. Bless someone who was kind to you, and forgive someone who wasn't."- Eileen Anglin

268. "Gratitude enables you to be fearless, and to never shy away from reveling in every moment of your life."
- Janice Anderson

269. "Those who complain much get little, those who complain little get much." - Jeanette Coron

270. "With grace and gratitude, life is filled with endless gladness." - Lailah Gifty Akita

271. "Your life is an opportunity to question, discover, and explore." - Janice Anderson

272. "Life is both beautiful and painful. In whatever situation we find ourselves in, no matter how unfortunate it may seem, there is always something to be thankful for – if we only choose to see it." - Frederick Espiritu

273. "Never let the things you want make you forget the things you have." - Sanchita Pandey

274. "Gratitude and attitude are notchallenges, they are choices."
- Robert Braath

275. "Gratitude opens our eyes… We are often praying for something God has already given us."- Steve Maraboli

276. "Gratitude is the seed of gladness."- Lailah Gifty Akita

277. "Gratitude has the power to fill your heart with love and your life with abundance." - Debasish Mridha

278. "Gratitude is the Single most important ingredient to living a successful and fulfilled life." - Jack Cranfield

279. "Don't count the days, Make the day count."
- Muhammad Ali

280. "Love yourself first to fill your heart with bliss. Now give it away with humility, love, and gratitude." - Debasish Mridha

281. "The real gift of gratitude – The more grateful you are, the more present you become." - Robert Holden

282. "To increase the value of your day, add some love and gratitude to your coffee and some kindness to your dinner."
- Debasish Mridha

283. "Gratitude is the gateway to a positive life." - A.D. Posey

284. "Gratitude is where every positive attitude starts."
- Michael Hyatt

285. "Your success should create a path that inspires others to follow." - Amitav Chowdhury

286. "A sign of gratitude is a thankful smile." - Debasish Mridha

287. "With grace and gratitude, great life evolves."
- Lailah Gifty Akita

288. "Start each day with thoughts of gratitude and you will attract the power of love." - Debasish Mridha

289. "Life is difficult for us all. We're all driven by love, and the desire to be loved and happy. If you take the right attitude, you think positively, you fill yourself with gratitude, joy and passion – it could be hell on earth and you'd still be happy."
- K.A. Hill

290. "It's not the joy that makes us grateful, its gratitude that makes us joyful." - Brother David Steindl-Rast

291. "When you realize nothing is lacking the whole world belongs to you." - Lao Tzu

292. "When you change the way you look at things, the things you look at change." - Wayne Dyer

293. When you practice gratefulness, there is a sense of respect for others." - The Dalai Lama

294. "Feeling gratitude and not expressing it is like wrapping a present and not giving it." - William Arthur Ward

295. "An attitude of gratitude fills a heart with happiness."
- Debasish Mridha

296. "Each day is a gift; open it with love and gratitude."
- Debasish Mridha

297. "An attitude of GRATITUDE, is life's most powerful affirmation" - Angie karan

298. "Gratitude is the vitamin of the soul." - Angie karan

299. "Never Kill your What Ifs,But first be Grateful for What Is." - Drishti Bablani

300. "With an attitude of gratitude, you can't go wrong. You are already putting it out there into the universe that you are ready to receive more. This is the universal truth. Be thankful for what you have. Your life is already abundant."
- Karen A. Baquiran

301. "Gratitude opens the door to the power, the wisdom, the creativity of the universe; you open the door through gratitude." - Deepak Chopra

302. "Gratitude is Riches, Complaint is Poverty." - Doris Day

303. "Let us not look back in anger, nor forward in fear, but around in awareness." - James Thurber

304. "Gratitude is an art of painting an adversity into a lovely picture." - Kak Sri

305. "Change your expectations for appreciation and the world changes instantly." - Tony Robbins

306. "Gratitude is not the result of things that happen to us, it is an attitude we cultivate by practice."- Alan Cohen

307. "Opportunities, relationships, even money flowed my way when I learned to be grateful no matter what happened in my life." - Oprah Winfrey

308. "Gratitude helps us to see what is there and what isn't." - Annette Bridges

309. "It's not what you gather but what you scatter that tells what kind of life you have lived." - Helen Walton

310. "No gesture is too small when done with gratitude." - Oprah Winfrey

311. "The miracle of gratitude is that it shifts your perception to such an extent that it changes the world you see." - Robert Holden

312. "Gratitude unlocks the fullness of life. It turns what we have into enough. And more. It turns denial into acceptance, chaos to order, confusion to clarity." - Melody Beattie

313. "You can have everything in life you want, if you will just help other people get what they want."- Zig Ziglar

314. "We often take for granted the very things that most deserve our gratitude." - Cynthia Ozick

315. "Your experience of life is not based on your life but on what you pay attention to." - Gregg Krech

316. "Do not take anything for granted not one smile or one breath, or one night in your cozy bed." - Terry Guillemets

317. "When we focus on our gratitude, the tide of disappointment goes out and the tide of love rushes in." - Kristin Armstrong

318. "Gratitude is not only the greatest of virtues, but the parent of all others." - Marcus Tullius Cicero

319. "Gratitude brings warmth to the giver and the receiver alike." - Robert D. Hales

320. "Gratitude unlocks the fullness of life. It turns what we have into enough, and more. It can turn a meal into a feast, a house into a home, a stranger into a friend." - Melody Beattie

321. "Today's gratitude buys tomorrow's happiness." - Michael McMillian

322. "One of the secrets of a long and fruitful life is to forgive everybody, everything, every night before you go to bed." - Bernard M. Baruch

323. "What can you do to promote world peace? Go home and love your family." - Mother Teresa

324. "The purpose of life is a life of purpose."- Robert Byrne

325. "Don't ask what the world needs. Ask what makes you come alive and then go and do that, because what the world

needs is people who have come alive." - Howard Martin

326. "God gave you a gift of 86,400 seconds today. Have you used one to say Thank You." - William Arthur Ward

327. "The deepest craving of human nature is the need to be appreciated." - William James

328. "Off with you! You're a happy fellow, for you'll give happiness and joy to many other people. There is nothing greater or better than that!"- Ludwig van Beethoven

329. "He is a wise man who does not grieve for the things for which he has not, but rejoices for those which he has." – Epictetus

330. "Things turn out the best for people who make the best of the way things turn out." - John Wooden

331. "Have the wisdom to perceive all there is to be thankful for, and then be thankful for the wisdom to perceive things so clearly." - Richelle E. Goodrich

332. "You cannot do a kindness too soon because you never know how soon it will be too late." - Ralph Waldo Emerson

333. "Gratitude is a currency that we can mint for ourselves, and spend without fear of bankruptcy." - Fred De Witt Van Amburgh

334. "If you count all your assets, you always show a profit." - Robert Brault

335. "We can only be said to be alive in those moments when our hearts are conscious of our treasures."- Thornton Wilder

336. "No one who achieves success does so without the help of others. The wise and confident acknowledge this help with gratitude." - Alfred North Whitehead

337. "The only people with whom you should try to get even are those who have helped you." - John E. Southard

338. "When I started counting my blessings my whole life turned around." - Willie Nelson

339. "Forget yesterday – it has already forgotten you. Don't sweat tomorrow – you haven't even met. Instead open your eyes and your heart to a truly precious gift – today."
- Steve Maraboli

340. "At times, our light goes out and is rekindled by a spark from another person. Each of us has caused to think with deep gratitude of those who have lightened the flame within us." - Albert Schweitzer

341. "If you want to make peace with your enemy, you have to work with your enemy. Then he becomes your partner."
- Nelson Mandella

342. "Gratitude is the smile of love." - Ralph Marston

343. "When you focus on gratitude the tide of disappointment goes out and the tide of love rushes in." - Kristin Armstrong

344. "Gratitude shifts your focus from what your life lacks to the abundance that is already present." - Marelisa Fábrega

345. "He who thanks but with the lips thanks but in part, the full, the true thanksgiving comes from the heart." - J.A. Shedd

346. "There is a calmness to a life lived in gratitude, a quite joy."
- Ralph H. Blum

347. "Real life isn't always going to be perfect or go our way, but the recurring acknowledgement of what is working in our lives can help us not only to survive but surmount our difficulties." - Sarah Ban Breathnach

348. "Silent gratitude isn't much use to anyone." - G.B. Stern

349. "Be grateful for who you are and what you will be."
- Lailah Gifty Akita

350. "Lead from the back – and let others believe they are in front." - Nelson Mandela

351. "A man is but the product of his thoughts. What he thinks he becomes." - Mahatma Gandhi

352. "Your life is your greatest teacher." - Oprah Winfrey

353. "As we express our gratitude, we must never forget that the highest appreciation is not to utter words, but to live by them." - John F. Kennedy

354. "Happiness cannot be travelled to, owned, worn or consumed. Happiness is the spiritual experience of living every minute with love, grace and gratitude."- Denis Waitley

355. "Gratitude can transform common days into thanksgivings, turn routine jobs into joy, and change ordinary opportunities into blessings." - William Arthur Ward

356. "Gratitude is the most exquisite form of courtesy."
- Jacques Maritain

357. "It is through gratitude for the present moment that the spiritual dimension of life opens up."- Eckhart Tolle

358. "There are only two ways to live your life. One is as though nothing is a miracle the other is as though everything is a miracle." - Albert Einstein

359. "The struggle ends when the gratitude begins."
- Neale Donald Walsch

360. "Gratitude is the best food and fuel to start the day for you. Have some at lunchtime and again at dinner too. It will energise and sustain you - the whole day through. But it will also leave you room, power and the thirst to do what you need to do and contribute." - Rasheed Ogunlaru

361. "An attitude of gratitude is one of the greatest attitudes of life." - Debasish Mridha M.D.

362. "Never forget to express your gratitude for the abundance and beauty of your life." - Debasish Mridha

363. "Your every positive action in your life will increase your self-esteem and this self-esteem will boost you for more positive action to take you on success"
- Rashedur Ryan Rahman

364. "When we begin to view our experiences through the lens of gratitude, our heart, mind and spirit naturally expand."
- David Brown Jr.

365. "If people begin to be more grateful, they will see the wonders of life." - Lailah Gifty Akita

REMEMBER:

"Focus on your daily blessings, future opportunities and possibilities, and never allow your challenges, struggles, and obstacles to interfere with your peace of mind. You owe abundant happiness and success to your inner-self."
- Edmond Mbiaka

THANK YOU